Having heard Dr. Ireland teach on prayer and then lead hundreds of men on their faces before God—me included—it was clear: He knew his way around God's throne room. *The Kneeling Warrior* will help you graduate from the College of Spiritual Warfare with an earned degree in PRAYER.

—TOMMY BARNETT
Author and senior pastor, Phoenix First Assembly of God
Chancellor, Southeastern University

Destiny comes to those who pray. For a church weak in the knees, the way up is down. David Ireland has written a powerful jeremiad on the upside of down and the power that comes to those "warriors" who will dare live "on a wing and a prayer." If you didn't believe this before, you'll believe this after reading *The Kneeling Warrior.* We don't know best when we're stretching on our tiptoes; we know best on our knees.

—LEONARD SWEET
Best-selling author, *The Gospel According to Starbucks*
Professor, Drew University and George Fox University
Chief contributor, Sermons.com

God uses David Ireland to communicate His Word with unusual passion and the anointing of the Holy Spirit.

—JIM CYMBALA
Author and senior pastor, The Brooklyn Tabernacle

A number of years ago during a study on prayer the Episcopal bishop of Massachusetts, Phillips Brooks, profoundly shared that: "Prayer is not the conquering of God's reluctance, but the taking hold of God's willingness." This statement has found its way into many books, including *Systematic Theology* by Augustus Strong. I have discovered that some books inspire, others educate, and some will motivate. A rare few will do all of these. *The Kneeling Warrior* is one of these. Dr. Ireland's insightful study on prayer deserves to be read while on your knees, then you won't have that far to go in order to implement the profound yet simple insights that will press you into embracing your assignment as a kneeling warrior. As his pastor for more than two decades, I am convinced of the validity of his own life of prayer, a life that flows out of this book and into our own hearts.

—Bishop Joseph L. Garlington, PhD
Senior Pastor, Covenant Church of Pittsburgh
Author, *Worship: The Pattern of Things in Heaven*

Dr. David Ireland has been an extraordinary leader and teacher on the subject of intercession. Few pastors have taught, modeled, and convened thousands of leaders around the centrality of intercession as well as Dr. Ireland. This book represents decades of lessons learned.

—Dr. Mac Pier
Author, *Spiritual Leadership in the Global City*
President, The NYC Leadership Center
Founder, Concerts of Prayer Greater New York

I remember meeting Dr. David Ireland for the first time almost two decades ago and saying to myself—that is a smart, Jesus-loving, highly organized, and gifted communicator of the gospel and leadership. Dr. Ireland's very diverse academic preparation as an engineer as well as a theologian allows him to do biblical architecture with complex issues of the Scripture. He's a man of integrity and obvious passion. He will bless, challenge, and encourage you regardless of the context. I highly recommend my friend Dr. David Ireland.

—DR. SAMUEL R. CHAND
Author, *Cracking Your Church's Culture Code*
www.samchand.com

Every teaching of Dr. Ireland gives you the detail and wisdom of a PhD but also the love and compassion of a child.

—KURT WARNER
Retired NFL Quarterback

the
KNEELING
WARRIOR

the
KNEELING
WARRIOR

DAVID D. IRELAND, PhD

CHARISMA
HOUSE

Most Charisma House Book Group products are available at special quantity discounts for bulk purchase for sales promotions, premiums, fund-raising, and educational needs. For details, write Charisma House Book Group, 600 Rinehart Road, Lake Mary, Florida 32746, or telephone (407) 333-0600.

The Kneeling Warrior by David D. Ireland, PhD
Published by Charisma House
Charisma Media/Charisma House Book Group
600 Rinehart Road
Lake Mary, Florida 32746
www.charismahouse.com

Unless otherwise noted, all Scripture quotations are from the Holy Bible, New International Version. Copyright © 1973, 1978, 1984, International Bible Society. Used by permission.

Scripture quotations marked nkjv are from the New King James Version of the Bible. Copyright © 1979, 1980, 1982 by Thomas Nelson, Inc., publishers. Used by permission.

Scripture quotations marked tlb are from The Living Bible. Copyright © 1971. Used by permission of Tyndale House Publishers, Inc., Wheaton, IL 60189. All rights reserved.

Cover design by Justin Evans
Design Director: Bill Johnson

Visit the author's website at www.davidireland.org.

Library of Congress Cataloging-in-Publication Data:
An application to register this book for cataloging has been
submitted to the Library of Congress.
International Standard Book Number: 978-1-62136-024-7
E-book ISBN: 978-1-62136-025-4

People and incidents in this book are composites created by the
author from his experiences in counseling. Names and details of the
stories have been changed, and any similarity between the names
and stories of individuals described in this book to individuals
known to readers is purely coincidental.

While the author has made every effort to provide accurate
telephone numbers and Internet addresses at the time of publication,
neither the publisher nor the author assumes any responsibility for
errors or for changes that occur after publication.

First edition

13 14 15 16 17 — 9 8 7 6 5 4 3 2 1
Printed in the United States of America

To the congregation of Christ Church,
who for over twenty-five years have
strived to make our church a house
of prayer for all nations.

Contents

Foreword

YOU ARE HOLDING AN AMAZING BOOK IN YOUR HANDS. You cannot possibly remain the same after you read it. It is written by one of the most brilliant pastors in America today. Dr. David Ireland has managed to produce a book that is simultaneously simple and profound, one that will teach you how to pray but also make you *want* to pray. It combines unpretentious scholarship, deep spirituality, and a transparent passion. It is a work of considerable research, quoting from the best-known people in church history to let you know that you are surrounded by the greatest of men and women when you want to be a person of prayer.

My mentor Dr. Martyn Lloyd-Jones introduced me to a Bible-reading plan that became pivotal in my own devotional life. Dr. Ireland's book will motivate you to have a strong prayer life that contains both the reading of the Bible and time spent alone with God. The result will be that you experience the presence of God in your daily devotional life and your walk with God. His goal for you is that you know the immediate presence of God. This book—if you follow it carefully—will lead you to experience precisely that. By drawing from the best prayer warriors of the past, David's book will help you to experience what the greatest saints have known—intimacy with God. What may attract you most of all is that anybody—even the weakest Christian—will be motivated to have a close walk with God that you never thought you could have.

Dr. David Ireland is one of most unusual men I have known. He is the pastor of the amazing Christ Church in the northern New Jersey area with campuses in and around Montclair, New Jersey. He and his wife, Marlinda, are what I can only call a "class act." He holds a PhD, and his wife will also shortly have an earned doctorate. Their church has enjoyed marvelous growth in a short period of time, reflecting a ministry that unashamedly upholds the Bible as the Word of God. But there is more; through his preaching there has been an ever-increasing sense of the presence of God in his own church. His ardent wish is to see true revival in his church and in the New York area. And yet that is what you can have a taste of—true revival in your heart—by reading this book.

One of the things I could not help but like most about David Ireland is our similarity of vision and goals. He has sought to make the preaching of the Word central alongside exciting worship and singing. He wants to combine the Word and the Spirit in his ministry—upholding sound evangelical teaching with the manifest power of the Holy Spirit. And there is yet another vision we have in common: he wants his church to reflect the same proportion of ethnicity and class of people that live in northern New Jersey. When I first preached for him, his church reminded me of Westminster Chapel.

I predict that this book will become a classic—ranking alongside the greatest books on prayer in church history. This book is God-honoring—a book that the devil will hate. As William Cowper put it, "Satan trembles when he sees the weakest saint upon his knees."

—Dr. R. T. Kendall

Minister, Westminster Chapel (1977–2002)

Introduction

SUCCESS IN LIFE CALLS FOR MILITANCY—SPIRITUAL militancy. Victory in the natural world requires triumph in the spiritual. Like it or not, a true Christian is called to fight. And there's too much to lose if we don't fight. Your destiny, your life's purpose, and the souls of those you influence are all hanging in the balance. They are desperately waiting for your victory cry to resound from the battlefield of life—the prayer closet. Your family's future, the place your children will take in society, and the promises of God must all be won through your prayers, fasting, and exercise of other biblical forms of spiritual warfare.

The great English preacher Charles H. Spurgeon said, "I take a promise and meditate upon it; I shake it to and fro, and sometimes the mellow fruit falls into my hand, at other times the fruit is less ready to fall, but I never leave off till I get it."[1] Yet the warrior instincts of many devout followers of Christ can grow dull. Sometimes we idly stand by while an evil tyrant pilfers our finances, snatches our health, destroys our marriages, and makes off with the promises of the God. Such spiritual complacency must be violently opposed. Otherwise the enemy of our souls will casually walk away with the very things God intended for us while we endure his victimization without a fight.

You use life insurance to protect your family and auto insurance to protect yourself as a driver, but think about what would happen if you used faith to protect the promises of God for your life. It's quite possible that you'd become a great threat to the kingdom of darkness and an even greater asset to the kingdom of light. If you're asking, "How do I use faith to protect God's promises?", the answer is found in this book!

Reading *The Kneeling Warrior* is an important step toward you becoming a champion for the promises of God. Like Abraham, Moses, Gideon, Ruth, and David, you are taking a stand to secure what God has for you. And this kind of dogged conviction is sure to bring you into the halls of victory alongside these spiritual champions—and even the obscure ones such as Simeon, Jephthah, and Esther. Each had two things in common: First, they did not tremble in the face of opposition. And second, they engaged in spiritual warfare to secure the things God had promised them.

FIGHTING IS IMPORTANT

The great Christian author C. S. Lewis said, "There is no neutral ground in the universe: every square inch, every split second is claimed by God and counterclaimed by Satan."[2] In other words, fighting spiritually is vital because of how invaluable God's promises are—and even the devil knows it.

The Bible outlines an amazing battle plan for regaining those things that have been snatched away by the enemy of our souls. After the Amalekites kidnapped the women and children and raided Ziklag—the place where David and the families of his six hundred men were living—he prayed, "Shall I pursue this raiding party?" Here's a paraphrase of God's answer: "Go and seize your stolen promises!" This riveting account of David's bravery in successfully recapturing the kidnapped families and their stolen property from the Amalekites did not come about by sheer military force. David used a threefold strategy. (See 1 Samuel 30.)

All heaven stands behind your spiritual efforts to regain your stolen promises— the gifts God has given to you.

First, he *engaged his feelings.* He grieved the loss of his family and property. He even had to work through his emotions regarding the threats his own men made to stone him because their families and property were stolen (v. 6). These wounded warriors thought that killing David would ease their pain. Thankfully David went to God in prayer to find the answer to his emotionally traumatic dilemma.

Second, *he engaged his faith*. When David prayed, "Shall I pursue this raiding party?", he was calling on God's wisdom to determine whether he should go after his family and property through military pursuit. David believed that God was the Captain of the army—a warring God—who would answer in a way that resulted in victory.

Third, David *engaged in a fight*. God's response to David's prayer came in the form of words. Yet those words were infused with power that fired David up for the battle. His mind was focused, knowing that God was on his side. And David was on God's side too. This battle was not only centered on revenge, but it was also fueled with marching orders directly from God. David was doing the Lord's work. Anytime you pursue God's promises, you are doing His work. All heaven stands behind your spiritual efforts to regain your stolen promises—the gifts God has given to you.

WHO SHOULD READ THIS BOOK?

The primary intention of *The Kneeling Warrior* is to equip you to regain God's promises for your life through spiritual warfare. As you learn to put your faith into action, you will adopt a biblical mind-set regarding spiritual warfare. This mind-set will position you to unleash spiritual weapons of mass destruction against our adversary regarding God's promises to you as outlined in Scripture. Establishing and maintaining a well-fortressed lifestyle will secure a spiritual legacy that will impact generations to come.

This book is written for those who want to take possession of all of the promises of God for their lives. That's you if you want God's will to be central to your life. Jesus taught us to pray this way: "Our Father in heaven, hallowed be your name, your kingdom come, your will be done on earth as it is in heaven" (Matt. 6:9–10). Pursuing and living God's will is the pinnacle of being a Christ-follower and key to accessing the promises of God.

This book is for you if you want to develop your knowledge and strength in the area of spiritual warfare. Paul said, "Finally, be strong in the Lord and in his mighty power. Put on the full armor of God so that you can take your stand against the devil's schemes" (Eph. 6:10–11). These words communicate your enlistment into the army of the Lord.

This book is for you if you are passionate about fulfilling the Great Commission. Jesus challenged us to "go and make disciples of all nations" (Matt. 28:19). The hope of seeing lost men and women come into God's kingdom hinges on your understanding of spiritual warfare. Paul shared: "The god of this age has blinded the minds of unbelievers, so that they cannot see the light of the gospel of the glory of Christ, who is the image of God" (2 Cor. 4:4). Salvation is what the Great Commission is all about. Often it is only through prayer and spiritual warfare that our family members, friends, and even our enemies come to experience the salvation found in Jesus Christ.

Finally this book is for you if you can no longer sit on the sidelines of the spiritual battle, hoping for a fair shake or wishing that Satan won't notice you. *The Kneeling Warrior* will equip you with the mind-set of a champion—one who is comfortable taking either an offensive or defensive stance against Satan. You want to become someone who's willing to pick spiritual fights with Satan or finish the ones he picks with you.

People I've worked with in developing a biblical framework of spiritual warfare have discovered answers to such probing questions as:

- How do I distinguish between trials and spiritual attacks?

- How do I fight for the promises of God?

- What's the distinction between the unbiblical name-it-and-claim-it theology and the scriptural mind-set that teaches me to seize my stolen promises?

- What exactly is spiritual warfare?

- What skills are needed to engage in spiritual warfare?

- Will engaging in spiritual warfare make me a Christian weirdo?

- How can I help others seize the promises of God for their lives?

THE BOOK'S PROMISE

The Kneeling Warrior offers a courageous how-to plan full of practical, spiritual tactics for reclaiming God's promises for your life. This book is about launching an all-out spiritual attack against the adversary to get back your career, to rekindle a satisfying marriage, to foster a healthy relationship with your kids, and to obtain any other promise worth recovering.

Very much like natural fighting, spiritual warfare demands training and strategy. Even understanding psychological warfare is crucial in gaining the upper hand against your adversary. The famed American general H. Norman Schwarzkopf warned that in case of war, psychological operations are "going to be absolutely a critical, *critical* part of any campaign that we must get involved in."[3] Similarly a solid understanding of biblical principles is essential to engage successfully in spiritual warfare.

The book is divided into three sections with the singular aim of equipping you to seize your stolen promises.

Very much like natural fighting, spiritual warfare demands training and strategy.

Part one focuses on *engaging your feelings.* It's time to wake up! The Lord's promises are well worth fighting for. God's kingdom is not Disneyland. It is miraculous, yes, but not dainty and magical. The promises of God don't just fall into your lap because you're a nice person. And when they do come into your possession, you have to activate the principles of faith to hold on to them. Contrary to popular belief, fighters don't hide their feelings. They own them. Warriors who successfully reclaim their prized possessions first place a high value on their feelings of anger, loss, or grief. Like David at Ziklag they become angry at the loss of a promise. They grieve over the unhealthy state of their marriage, their waning career, or the broken relationship with their children.

Engaging your feelings is the first stage in launching an all-out attack to regain the things the enemy has stolen from you. If your loss doesn't bother you enough to fight for it, then you will simply shrug your shoulders and chalk it up to the will of God. But giving up so easily could be a regretful mistake.

Part two teaches you how to *engage your faith.* Every believer in God's kingdom holds dual citizenship. We are both worshippers *and* warriors. The claim that we are called to be worshippers is seldom debated because, after all, worship is fun. It's enjoyable. With a passport labeled "worship" I travel to all the cool vacation spots. My other passport—the one that grants me passage into the war zones of life—is seldom used because the travel spots there are messy and unruly. Yet the Bible emphatically declares, "The LORD is a warrior" (Exod. 15:3), and "Praise be to the LORD my Rock, who trains my hands for war, my fingers for battle" (Ps. 144:1).

Spiritual warfare permeates throughout the Bible. From the Old Testament to the New, believers wrestled forces of evil and wickedness to seize God's promises. Yet modern-day Christians—even in do-or-die confrontations with horrific calamities like global economic ruin and the moral erosion of society—are reticent to fight back. Instead many choose to cower to forces like an unhealthy family life and miserable careers. Some Christians, with a distorted view of God, think He's simply a meek, mild-mannered deity who only governs in the area of morality, shying away from fighting for ownership beyond the scope of ethics. This thinking is one-dimensional and limited to the full nature of God. Perhaps they simply don't want to fight or they don't yet know how.

A lifestyle of faith is not a passive one. Engaging your faith—the faith outlined in the Bible—produces the characteristics of a kneeling warrior. True biblical faith emboldens you. It infuses you with courage that empowers you to declare to the enemy of your soul, "I'm mad, and I'm not going to take it anymore!"

The third part of the book offers practical instructions on how to *engage in the fight.* "What would Jesus do?" We've seen this catchy phrase on T-shirts, hats, tattoos, and bumper stickers. But when it comes to actually defending the will of God, the Bible answers this piercing question the same way time after time: Jesus would fight! And if He used the Word as a weapon to defeat Satan, shouldn't we do the same—rather than backing down?

> **True biblical faith emboldens you. It infuses you with courage that empowers you to declare to the enemy of your soul, "I'm mad, and I'm not going to take it anymore!"**

As warriors we must keep ourselves in top fighting condition by practicing spiritual disciplines. This section outlines the workout regimen that can transform even the wimpiest of spiritual fighters into aggressive, lean, mean spiritual warfare machines. You will learn the power of fasting and prayer-intercession as weapons in warfare. You will enjoy the victory found in meditation, reflection, and solitude. *The Kneeling Warrior* will help you discover the liberty associated with travailing in prayer. You will also discover the peace found in knowing your identity in Christ.

A KEY CALLED PROMISE

In Bunyan's great allegory *The Pilgrim's Progress* the character Christian decides to leave the main highway and follow another path that seemed easier. But this path leads him into the territory of Giant Despair, who owns Doubting-Castle. Eventually he is captured by Giant Despair and kept in a dungeon. He is advised to kill himself. The Giant said there was no use trying to keep on with his journey. For the time it seemed as if Despair had really conquered Christian. But then Hope, Christian's companion, comes to remind him of previous victories.

It eventually came about that on Saturday, about midnight, they began to pray and continued until almost morning. Now a little before it was day, Christian broke out in passionate speech: "What a fool...am I, thus to lie in a stinking Dungeon, when I may as well walk at liberty? I have a Key in my bosom, called *Promise*, that will, (I am persuaded) open any lock in Doubting-Castle." Then said Hopeful, "That's good news, good brother, pluck it out of thy bosom, and try." And the prison gates flew open.[4]

The Kneeling Warrior contains the key that will throw open the gates to the promises of God Satan has stolen and locked away from you. But it will require a fight on your part. This is a fight that will impact your destiny, the welfare and salvation of your family, and the souls of others God has called you to influence. Your feet are now planted on the battleground. You are entering your training to go and seize the promises of God for your life. I have no doubt that you will arise victorious. Enjoy the read, mighty warrior.

PART ONE

ENGAGE
YOUR FEELINGS

THE MAKING OF A
KNEELING WARRIOR

FIVE YEARS AGO A SINGLE NIGHT'S DREAM TAUGHT ME more about prayer than six years of seminary—even after two decades of serving as a pastor. Like many Christians I believed that my prayer life was satisfactory. But God had a different opinion. Sounds strange, right? After all, I am a preacher. Each week I share God's Word with thousands of spiritually hungry people. They come to me for biblical insight and for tools to help them build stronger relationships with God. But one fitful night the Lord showed me His perspective of my prayer life and what He wanted me to do about it.

I dreamed I was working in an office complex surrounded by woods and wildlife. As I left the building and walked into the bright daylight, I was aware that a few members of my staff had stayed behind in the office. To my surprise, large birds of prey—hawks and vultures—were lying wounded or dead outside the building. It was a frightening scene. These large majestic birds were scattered everywhere, lying defeated and limply strewn on a bed of rocks. It was clear I was in the middle of a war zone where the birds had been engaged in mortal combat and had lost.

> **Through prayer we regain our strength
> to defeat the enemy and accomplish
> the will of God for our generation.**

Suddenly I noticed an eagle wedged between the rocks—seemingly hiding and extremely exhausted. It shivered in an effort to regain its strength. It was tucked so deeply in the cleft of the rock that the hawks and vultures could not see it. I wondered what had killed all these fierce birds and quickly realized it was the eagle that had defeated all of its attackers. Then I saw the eagle mount up with a ferocious squawk. As it flew over the bed of rocks, it snatched a hawk and carried it high into the sky. Although the hawk struggled for its life, it could not get free from the eagle's sharp and powerful talons. Within moments the eagle sunk its sharp beak into the neck of the hawk. As I watched this scene, trying to figure out what was going on, the eagle removed its beak from the neck of the hawk, lifted up the hawk's wing, and thrust its beak into the hawk's heart to kill it.

Seeing this, I quickly ran back into the office to get my executive pastor and show him this once-in-a-lifetime scene, but I couldn't find him. I looked in the office of one of the associate pastors, and he wasn't there either. I picked up the closest phone and called a second associate pastor. He answered the phone but was hesitant when I urged him to meet me quickly in my office. In the dream it was so clear: this pastor wasn't in a good place spiritually. His fire for prayer had dimmed so much that he couldn't detect the urgency of the moment. It was clear to me that his spiritual antenna had become terribly dull. Though he was a good man, he was completely oblivious to the activities of the Holy Spirit and the dynamics of spiritual warfare. I gave up urging him to come because it was of no use. And with that the dream ended abruptly. I awoke shaken to my core, so I immediately sought the Lord for the interpretation of this dream.

Here's what God revealed: the jagged rocks signify the spiritual warfare we all face. The eagle represents the Christian who's been tired and seemingly defeated from life's battles. The hawks and vultures are the demons working to destroy society and the lives of individuals in it, but their lying wounded and dead are signs of their defeat. God was letting me see how the powers of the enemy will be conquered as the eagles regain their strength to fight the good fight of faith. The key was the eagle's need to retreat between the rocks to regain its fighting strength. Hiding in the cleft of the rocks is symbolic of prayer and waiting upon the Lord (Isa. 40:29–31). Through prayer we regain our strength to defeat the enemy and accomplish the will of God for our generation.

After gaining these insights from God, I knew He wanted more from me. I knew simply being a man who prays wasn't enough. God was saying, "David, I want you to be a man *of* prayer."

You may be wondering what the difference is between a man who prays and a man of prayer. The difference is that being a man of prayer is to become a kneeling warrior—someone who prays with the fierce intensity of a prizefighter and beats down the obstacles set up by the enemy to hinder God's purpose and the quality of life He has called us to experience.

I crafted the phrase *kneeling warrior* after learning how the great statesman Daniel fought and defeated the severe atrocities of his era by praying three times a day (Dan. 6:10). He knew that the power of prayer could defeat the most severe demonic oppression and inhumane treatment of God's highest creation, humanity. Further, Daniel modeled how kneeling warriors can be stationed in the upper echelons of government, as he was, yet remain humble before God without viewing prayer as a lowly function or duty.

Champions aren't made in gyms. Champions are made from something they have deep inside them—a desire, a dream, a vision.

Studying Daniel made me even more determined. Becoming a kneeling warrior meant more to me than earning my PhD.

It became more impressive to me than writing books or even building a thriving church. As I heard the heart and voice of the Lord and understood what He was calling me to do, I wept, knowing deeply that my life was about to be transformed completely. I knew I had to reevaluate, reprioritize, and reorganize all of my responsibilities as a husband, father, and pastor to become the kneeling warrior God was calling me to be. The hours between 4:00 a.m. and 6:00 a.m., which I had designated as sacred, were to be guarded more than ever as one of the times I would man my battle station daily as a kneeling warrior.

Do You Have the Will to Become a Kneeling Warrior?

As a boy I admired the confidence and conviction of Muhammad Ali, who is not a Christian but was deeply insightful regarding the mentality of effective fighters. Once, to psych out a challenger for the heavyweight title, Ali said, "Champions aren't made in gyms. Champions are made from something they have deep inside them—a desire, a dream, a vision. They have to have last-minute stamina, they have to be a little faster; they have to have the skill, and the will. But the will must be stronger than the skill."[1]

Applying Ali's wisdom to the modern-day church—rife with great preachers and teachers and filled with great writers and singers—we similarly need strong kneeling warriors who have a burning desire to bring the burdens of a hurting world before a loving God in prayer. After the Spirit-filled sermon is done and the powerful praise and worship have ended in our churches, what are we really doing for God? I want to be named among that distinguished group of warriors who have both the skill and the will to defeat the enemy's schemes. That's why I answered the call to become a kneeling warrior.

And answering the call is far deeper than saying, "I'm going to pray more for myself, my family, my career, and my ministry." It is about wholly engaging your feelings in the spiritual battle because it has become crystal clear to you that something *must* be done. Sitting idly by while Satan pillages your family, steals God's promises from this generation, and destroys humanity's hope for a just society is too high a price to pay. Becoming a kneeling warrior is the only sound conclusion you can draw from this spiritual dilemma. So, what do you do? You willingly embrace the counsel Paul gave to his spiritual son, Timothy, when he wrote: "Endure hardship with us like a good soldier of Christ Jesus" (2 Tim. 2:3). If you limit this verse as private counsel from Paul to Timothy, you miss the essential truth of these powerful words. You must embrace the passage as guidance for your own life such that fighting becomes your choice, and you willingly enlist yourself as an unwavering soldier of Christ Jesus.

Like Muhammad Ali, do you have a desire, dream, or vision? Do you have the stamina—and more importantly, a will that is stronger than skill—to become a champion of prayer? Do you have what it takes to become a kneeling warrior? Before you step foot on the battlefield, your thoughts and feelings must echo the words of the apostle Paul: "I can do all things through Christ who strengthens me" (Phil 4:13, NKJV). Kneeling warriors consciously—even subconsciously—develop the behavior of champions.

A kneeling warrior is emboldened by a passionate reason to fight. No one enters into warfare without a just cause or a feeling of righteous anger. Those feelings become the fuel of persistence when the battle intensifies. What's driving your passion to become a kneeling warrior? Is it a difficult trial? Are you experiencing some sort of barrenness in your life? Perhaps the deafening cry of humanity bound for a Christ-less eternity has gripped your soul. Kneeling warriors are so personally troubled by pain or the injustices of our fallen society that they take the posture of prayer to tear down strongholds designed by Satan to thwart the purposes of God.

The kneeling warrior enters onto the battlefield of prayer when he realizes that he has skin in the game. There is too much at stake if he does not get a real breakthrough from God. This was the case with Larry, a man who came to Christ after years of living in sexual confusion and sin. Larry longed to feel whole again, but a large cyst on his back—the result of some risqué sexual behavior—was a constant reminder of his past. Doctors had told him that removing it would leave a huge scar.

> **Kneeling warriors are so personally troubled by pain or the injustices of our fallen society that they take the posture of prayer to tear down strongholds designed by Satan to thwart the purposes of God.**

It's God's desire to help everyone experience a breakthrough in prayer. A few years ago I took Christ Church through

Operation Take Back, a forty-day spiritual journey aimed at helping participants reclaim areas of their lives that had been damaged or lost through sin and spiritual neglect.

During Operation Take Back Larry prayed and asked God for a miracle. A few weeks later, during a routine physical, a new doctor told Larry he could remove the growth with no scarring. After the surgery even the doctor was surprised at how completely the area healed. Larry told of God's faithfulness, saying, "That cyst removal has so many spiritual implications. I'm even more amazed at God's love for me." Suffice it to say, Larry became a kneeling warrior because he needed to have all signs of his past sexual brokenness removed. The skin in the game for Larry was seeing God remove the cyst from his back. God did it, and Larry emerged as a kneeling warrior.

Kneeling warriors are made in the crucible of difficulty. These men and women haven't been born spiritual champions. They didn't always have power with God. They *became* spiritual champions by emerging from the belly of trials armed with the newfound mentality of soldiers. And similar to natural fighters, kneeling warriors must win the battle psychologically before they can enter the ring to contend for the prize.

It wasn't until Hannah rejected her own self-pity and confusion and embraced her passion for having a son that God opened her womb. Samuel, Israel's great prophet, was in the mind of God since the beginning of time. Yet the nation could not benefit from his gift until his barren mother turned her tears of sorrow and self-pity into liquid prayers. Before Samuel was naturally conceived, he was birthed in the womb of prayer. The words capturing that precious moment, when Hannah's liquid prayers were poured out are, "In bitterness of soul Hannah wept much and prayed to the LORD. And she made a vow, saying, 'O LORD Almighty, if you will only look upon your servant's misery and remember me, and not forget your servant but give her a son, then I will give him to the LORD for all the days of his life'" (1 Sam. 1:10–11). Hannah's passion for a son turned her into a kneeling warrior.

Throughout the Bible Jacob is portrayed as a man with a deceptive streak. Yet his passion to fulfill God's call on his life caused him to emerge as an awesome intercessor. Faced with the threat of being murdered by his brother, Esau, whom he had twice deceived some two decades earlier, Jacob spent the night in prayer. The picture of intercession the Bible paints for us is Jacob wrestling all night with an angel of the Lord (Gen. 32:22–32). The stakes were high. If Jacob didn't prevail with God, he would be killed by Esau. Jacob's passion was captured while wrestling with the angel, when he said, "I will not let you go unless you bless me" (v. 26). This ordinary man, known by his flawed character, became a kneeling warrior when his agonizing passion for life drove him to cry out to God.

The famed Scottish preacher Robert Murray M'Cheyne became a powerful kneeling warrior before he slipped into eternity at the young age of twenty-nine—just seven years after entering the ministry. He answered the call to live for Christ shortly after his older brother David died an untimely death. David had prayed repeatedly for Robert's conversion, and Robert later acknowledged that the Holy Spirit used his brother's death to carve a deep impression on his soul. In a July 8, 1842, letter to a friend M'Cheyne wrote: "This day eleven years ago, I lost my loved and loving brother, and began to seek a Brother who cannot die."[2] Following his conversion, M'Cheyne's passion to see lost people meet the Savior resulted in a tremendous revival in Dundee, Scotland, at the Church of St. Peter. Unbelievers came in droves to hear and see this preacher who had wept for their conversion. Since his death visitors from the Commonwealth, the United States, and Europe come to stand in the pulpit that is said to have been wet with his tears as he urged people to commit their lives to Christ.[3]

THE SPIRIT OF A WARRIOR

Whether you know it or not, as a Christ-follower you are already engaged in spiritual warfare—regardless of your level of participation. If you choose to merely sit in the stands and watch the fight, you're still in the battle. Don't be fooled! You are not just a spectator; you are a casualty. There is a better option. You can arm yourself with the Scriptures and engage in the battle. Paul emphatically warned the Ephesians about this high-stakes battle when he told them:

> Finally, be strong in the Lord and in his mighty power. Put on the full armor of God so that you can take your stand against the devil's schemes. For our struggle is not against flesh and blood, but against the rulers, against the authorities, against the powers of this dark world and against the spiritual forces of evil in the heavenly realms. Therefore put on the full armor of God, so that when the

day of evil comes, you may be able to stand your
ground.

—EPHESIANS 6:10–13

Spiritual warfare is not biblical semantics. It embodies
the idea that there is an ongoing high-stakes war between
the kingdom of God and the kingdom of evil. This dualism
between good and evil did not always exist, because God alone
existed in the beginning (Gen. 1:1). He is the epitome of goodness, love, and righteousness. Evil was born in eternity past
when Lucifer—one of God's angels—decided to rebel against
God (Ezek. 28:11–17). God evicted Lucifer from heaven, along
with a number of angels who aligned themselves with his rebel-
lion. His fate of eternal banishment from the presence of God
and everlasting punishment in hell awaits him somewhere in
the future (Rev. 20:7–10). In the meantime the dualism of good
and evil, light and darkness, and right and wrong continues as
a point of contention in every generation.

**Whether you know it or not, as a Christ-follower
you are already engaged in spiritual warfare—
regardless of your level of participation.**

Lucifer, who's also known as Satan, the deceiver, the devil,
Beelzebub, and a number of other biblical titles, established a
kingdom that is constantly at war with all that is good, holy,
and associated with the kingdom of God. Humanity—believers
and unbelievers alike—is included in this age-old battle simply
because we are God's most prized creation. The term *spiritual*

warfare describes this ongoing conflict between Satan's kingdom and God's kingdom.

This adversary is by no means equal in power, wisdom, or strategy to God. Yet God, in His infinite wisdom, allows Satan to engage in his treacherous schemes. The only plausible theological reason for God allowing such activity is that His will is still being executed in all things concerning all people. God is the only One who is omnipotent, omniscient, and omnipresent. Satan is a defeated foe who is a constant source of irritation in the grand scheme of things. Though he's an irritant, he is a formidable nuisance to the human race.

To become equipped for such a high-stakes war, we must become skilled in spiritual warfare to destroy Satan's plans for this generation. Because Satan's annihilation can only occur when God casts him into hell, each generation must enlist in the battle to defeat this hellish foe. Ignoring the realities of this spiritual war means likely forfeiting some of God's best promises for your life and family. Your destiny and that of your children are put at risk if you plead ignorance to the age-old battle between good and evil.

CHOOSING TO ENLIST IN THE BATTLE

The Bible is clear on God's call for all believers to become kneeling warriors. Still, many dutiful Christians don't know how to do so. Here's what Paul told the Corinthians:

> For though we live in the world, we do not wage
> war as the world does. The weapons we fight with
> are not the weapons of the world. On the contrary,

they have divine power to demolish strongholds.
We demolish arguments and every pretension that
sets itself up against the knowledge of God, and we
take captive every thought to make it obedient to
Christ.

—2 CORINTHIANS 10:3–5

It seems like a no-brainer to see that the instant you
embrace the salvation Jesus freely offers, you are to jump right
smack into the heat of the battle. I believe Paul's words are
taken so lightly because fighting is such hard work. It is not
sophisticated or intellectual. It is dirty. It's primitive, instinc-
tive, and inherently risky. Many Christians limit their spiritual
activities to the safety of more dignified pursuits. They erroneously believe that simply attending weekly church services and
reading the Bible will keep them safe. And while these are good
activities and ones they can easily handle, they don't qualify as
full-fledged spiritual warfare.

> **Ignoring the realities of this spiritual
> war means likely forfeiting some of God's
> best promises for your life and family.**

Kneeling warriors are spurred by passion. Their will to
fight is borne from feelings of lack or pain. David, who was a
musical teenager tasked with herding sheep, became a mighty
warrior after a ferocious lion stole one of the sheep from his
flock. When that happened, something rose up in David that
caused him to contend for his property. Those were *his* sheep.

He was the only one who had to give an account to his dad if he returned home with fewer sheep than he was assigned to shepherd. That warrior's calling was further confirmed when a bear attempted to carry off another one of the sheep from the flock. David confronted the attacker and regained his sheep. So when David finally met Goliath—this nine-foot giant of a man—his warrior instincts had already been awakened. David said to King Saul, "Let no one lose heart on account of this Philistine; your servant will go and fight him" (1 Sam. 17:32). And fight him he did.

David spoke like a true warrior when he attempted to bolster the feelings of Saul's troops by telling them *not to lose heart*. The call to fight Goliath called for the same feelings David exhibited when fighting the lion and the bear. There must be something important at stake to pique your emotions toward warfare. For David, defeating Goliath was a personal victory. He was appalled that Goliath dared "defy the armies of the living God" (v. 26). Similarly, when you feel the personal loss of pride, promise, destiny, or some other thing you deem valuable, a fight will arise in you. David voluntarily chose to fiercely defend God's people and God's great name.

We all know that God does not force anyone to love Him. In the same way, He does not force anyone to pray. Prayer is a completely voluntary undertaking. Thumb through the Gospels, and you'll notice that Jesus never initiated training in the arena of prayer. Instead He modeled prayer by being a man of prayer Himself. Jesus offered instruction in the art of prayer only when His disciples *asked*, "Lord, teach us to pray" (Luke 11:1). Moved by a personal need for power with God and help for their generation, the plea for instruction in prayer was humbly voiced by the disciples. Thus it's easy to deduce that kneeling warriors become inducted into Jesus's school of prayer when they personally recognize their own powerlessness resulting from prayerlessness. This revelation drives them to their knees, awakening them to the need for a life of prayer.

IT'S TIME TO ENLIST!

David's decision to develop a life of prayer, leading him to become a kneeling warrior, occurred in hard times. Years after David's defeat of Goliath King Saul's jealousy toward him drove David to live sixteen months in the Philistine country town of Ziklag (1 Sam. 27:6–7). Having received permission from Achish, king of the Philistines, to live there with his six hundred men and their families, David came face-to-face with the fundamental need for prayer. One day while David and his troops were on a mission, the Amalekites attacked Ziklag and set the city on fire. David's wives and the wives and children of his men were kidnapped by this vicious raiding party (1 Sam. 30:1–2).

> **When you feel the personal loss of pride, promise, destiny, or some other thing you deem valuable, a fight will arise in you.**

The sudden loss of his family and the anguished hopelessness of his men led David into a state of emotional isolation. His feelings of discouragement and failure were compounded by his own men's threats to stone him in response to their anger and grief. I'm sure they thought, "How could David, this military genius, leave Ziklag unprotected while we went off on our mission? Why didn't he think to leave a few dozen men behind to protect the women and children?" Their only comfort came from talking about stoning David. In their eyes he was to blame.

David was forced to find comfort in God—the One who was with him years ago when a lion and a bear stole off with a sheep from the flock one starry night. Scripture declares, "But David found strength in the LORD his God" (1 Sam. 30:6). The word *strength* in this verse is the Hebrew word *chazaq* (pronounced *khaw-zak*), which was used to describe battle scenes that called for a courageous response. It means to help, be strong, to repair, to restrain, and to encourage. When David turned to the Lord, his emotional state of helplessness and despair was restored to that of courage and might.

Even after receiving God's reassurance, comfort, and encouragement, David wanted more. He inquired of the Lord: "'Shall I pursue this raiding party? Will I overtake them?' 'Pursue them,' he [the Lord] answered. 'You will certainly overtake them and succeed in the rescue'" (v. 8). David's sense of loss and the pain of knowing what atrocities, including rape, awaited his wives and the families of his six hundred men fueled his prayers.

Until you experience the personal loss or are fueled by the threat of losing your own family, destiny, or some other invaluable item, you'll continue to view enlisting into the school of prayer as optional to your Christian walk. You must wholeheartedly agree that the promises of God are worth fighting for—that they're worth *you* fighting for. They will only come into your possession because you have coupled the principles of faith with the art of spiritual warfare.

A woman in my church, Phyllis, had lived with constant financial stress while raising two children whose deadbeat dad contributed only occasionally for birthday and Christmas presents. She wanted to trust God, but she felt such anger toward her ex-husband that it was difficult to maintain faith. During my teaching on prayer and fasting, Phyllis decided to seek God's help with renewed passion. There were low points, when Phyllis's anger flared against her ex, but she maintained a season of prayer and fasting to give her faith in God a chance. Phyllis was pleasantly surprised when, after only a few days, her ex-husband contacted her out of the blue to say he was going to be sending child support payments every two weeks. In fact, he wanted the necessary information to have the payments directly deposited into her bank account to avoid any lateness on his part. Phyllis's e-mail to me concluded with this state-ment: "I now know that the prayers of the righteous avail much with God." Had Phyllis maintained prayerlessness concerning her children's child support, she wouldn't have experienced this awesome miracle.

> **You must wholeheartedly agree that the promises of God are worth fighting for— that they're worth *you* fighting for.**

Jessie Penn-Lewis, the great Scottish intercessor who played an integral role in birthing the Welsh Revival of 1904–1905, wrote: "In the war upon the powers of darkness, prayer is the...mightiest weapon." The role of prayer in that day was "in (1) aggressive war upon them [principalities] and their works; (2) in the deliverance of men from their power; and (3) against them as a hierarchy of powers opposed to Christ and His Church."[4] Lewis's feelings of anger toward her nation's condition of spiritual apathy and lukewarmness of soul drove her to her knees. The result was a mighty outpouring of the Holy Spirit that swept thousands of people into the kingdom of God.

FIGHTING IS NOT OPTIONAL!

Engaging your feelings is the first stage in launching an all-out attack to regain the valuable things the enemy has stolen from you. If your loss doesn't bother you enough to fight, then you'll simply chalk up the loss to being one of life's unfortunate tragedies. But that conclusion may be far from the truth.

The most powerful action you can take is to bend your knees in prayer.

Yes, David and his men recaptured their families from the Amalekites, but what would have happened to those women and children if David hadn't prayed? What would have become of David's reputation and that of his fighting men had they returned to Israel without their families? It's probable that he would have lost the respect of the nation and become the brunt of piercing sarcasm regarding his status as a warrior.

David's feelings triggered him to pray a warfare prayer. He

sought God's advice about pursuing the marauding party. And God did not hesitate to answer, "Pursue them." To enlist in the army of the Lord, you have to acknowledge God as a fighter. Equally important is the fact that your loss or potential loss must be so valuable that it drives you toward massive action. The most powerful action you can take is to bend your knees in prayer.

While away at college my daughter, Jessica, walked with a few friends back to the dorms after having dinner at a local restaurant. Cars at the intersection were waiting for the traffic light to turn green. Suddenly a driver threw his car into park and yelled out at the top of his voice, "My bike!" Apparently he had spotted a guy riding his bicycle that was stolen the day before. The thief heard his scream and started to peddle off as fast as he could. As the girls watched, the driver chased him down, shoved him off the bike, and walked his bike back to his car. After he threw the bike in the back seat, the light turned green and he drove away. His stolen bike was valuable enough for him to take action. In the same way you cannot sit idly by chalking up the enemy's robberies to life's unfortunate moments or the will of God. Get mad! Take action! Become like David and that motorist. Go get your stuff back!

How Do You See God?

The standard answers most people give to the question "What's God like?" range from loving, merciful, and gracious to patient, long-suffering, and righteous. All of these answers are absolutely correct, yet they are incomplete. David's view of God was not limited to His being meek and mild. The physical and emotional welfare of hundreds of women and children hung on his prayer. He viewed God as the consummate warrior who would not hesitate to answer if an earthly warrior's prayer arose to His throne.

Further, David's view of God wasn't limited to that of an earthly parent who simply coddles His children when they are hurting. Our God comforts, but He is not afraid to forcefully confront evil or unrighteousness. Thankfully David was able to identify that quality in our God. David viewed God's role in our lives beyond the parameters of rendering decisions on matters of morality and ethics. He didn't view God strictly as a resident policeman who settled arguments with words. David saw God as the One who would sanction his cry for street justice. Thus God's direct response to David's prayer was, "Pursue them."

David viewed God as a warrior (Exod. 15:3) who was equally comfortable on the battlefield as He was in the sanctuary. God is the commander of the army of the Lord, and a warfare prayer was in order (Josh. 5:14). David's theology supported spiritual warfare. Similarly your prayers stem from the way you view God.

Several years ago I was leaving my office at the church one afternoon. Just before I pushed open the double doors to exit the building, to my surprise the doors suddenly opened from the outside. I was startled because a huge guy was suddenly facing me. I was standing two steps above him, yet I was only nearing the height of his chest. Not only was he tall, but also he was wide. Plus he was unusually buff. Looking at him, I felt like I was looking at a gladiator from the first century. His neck was big and sinewy. His biceps were burgeoning from his already large shirt. Before I could say a word, his deep baritone voice belted out the words: "Hey, Pastor, good to see you." I relaxed knowing that he recognized me and knew my status, though I had never seen him before. His warm smile also helped calm my nerves.

> **Our heavenly Father wants us to seek Him in every capacity of His divinity.**

He introduced himself as a member of my congregation and explained that he had come to the church to drop off a package for someone on my staff. He also told me that he was a professional heavyweight boxer and was flying to Las Vegas on Thursday for a fight. He said, "Would you mind praying for me?" I thought, "How do you pray for someone whose job it is to beat up other big men? Do you lay hands on him when you pray? Will he misinterpret my pastoral touch as an invitation to spar?" These thoughts raced through my mind as I stood in front of this giant of a man. Then I quickly concluded: a warrior needs a warfare prayer!

So I prayed, "God, anoint Your son that he may knock out his opponent. Give him the tenacity of a warrior when he enters the ring. Let Thursday be a glorious day of victory. In Jesus's name, amen." He was pleased, and I walked to my car with a smile on my face. Weeks later I saw him in church and had to ask about the outcome. His face beamed as he shared the news: "I won! Thanks for the prayer." I walked away knowing that our heavenly Father wants us to seek Him in every capacity of His divinity. He is a comforter. He is a merciful God. And, at the same time, He is the Almighty Warrior. Learn to pray more warfare prayers so that you can lay claim to God's promises for your life and the lives of those around you.

HOW DO YOU SEE YOURSELF?

You picked up this book for a specific reason. You want to be trained in the art of spiritual warfare. That is a noble goal, and through the help of the Holy Spirit this goal will be accomplished. Any threat you may be facing right now regarding the loss of something valuable will be averted as you seek the help of God.

You must see yourself as a warrior in the making. Each exploit will build your faith. But your warfare training begins in your mind. That is why Paul told young Timothy, "Endure hardship with us like a good soldier of Christ Jesus" (2 Tim. 2:3). You are to take the viewpoint of a solider as you serve Christ. And while there are hardships and difficulties in maintaining your vigilance in spiritual warfare, the prizes of safeguarding the promises of God and leading people into a relationship with Him are worth it all.

Like Paul, kneeling warriors also have bragging rights. At the end of his spiritual journey Paul wrote: "I have fought the good fight, I have finished the race, I have kept the faith" (2 Tim. 4:7). Not everyone can say that they have fought a good fight, much less finished the race with their faith intact. Mastering spiritual warfare is a highly prized goal.

One of the fiercest branches of the US military is the Navy SEALS. They live by a code that begins with these words:

> In times of war or uncertainty there is a special breed of warrior ready to answer our Nation's call. A common man with uncommon desire to succeed. Forged by adversity, he stands alongside America's finest special operations forces to serve his country, the American people, and protect their way of life. I am that man.[5]

They see themselves as unique warriors ready for battle. This code unifies all Navy SEALS into a cohesive community of fierce fighters. It reinforces *why* each became a SEAL and *how* a SEAL is to function while enrolled in the armed services. This code serves as a rallying cry for all when tough times occur.

Prayer starts in your feelings and thoughts about God, His power, His willingness to act, and your willingness to believe that His promises are absolutely attainable through prayer.

I took some editorial liberties and contextualized the code for the kneeling warrior when I trained my congregation in the art of spiritual warfare. Here's the perspective we ought to embrace to answer God's call to be a good solider of Christ Jesus:

> In times of spiritual warfare and uncertainty there is a special breed of warrior ready to answer the call

to prayer. A common believer with an uncommon desire to succeed. Forged by adversity, I stand alongside God's finest kneeling warriors to serve His kingdom, the human race, and protect their way of life. I am that warrior.

I will never quit. I persevere and thrive on adversity. God's kingdom expects me to be spiritually harder and mentally stronger than my enemies. If knocked down, I will get back up, every time. I will draw on every remaining ounce of strength to protect fellow believers and to accomplish our mission. I am never out of the fight.

Isn't this the perspective our commander in chief, Jesus, taught us to have? Jesus said to His disciples, "They should always pray and not give up" (Luke 18:1). This command *to never give up* embodies the attitude and will a kneeling warrior must possess before he bends his knees in prayer. Prayer starts in your feelings and thoughts about God, His power, His willingness to act, and your willingness to believe that His promises are absolutely attainable through prayer.

Chapter 2

DON'T RING THE BELL!

T HE NAVY SEALS STORMED THE SECRET COMPOUND of the infamous terrorist Osama bin Laden in a remote area of Pakistan in May 2011. Within forty minutes they found and killed this mastermind of evil and were back on their helicopter headed for safety. But these guys didn't become fierce fighting machines overnight.

The first phase of training to be a Navy SEAL lasts a grueling eight weeks. Midway through this rigorous basic conditioning session comes *Hell Week*. The intensity ratchets up significantly during this ultimate test of mental, physical, and emotional strength. Candidates only get 4 hours of sleep during the 132-hour period. And they are wet and cold the entire time. They are required to swim through mud, push logs up sand hills, and carry boats with their bare hands, all while dealing with chafing, bleeding, open sores and tired muscles.

To compound the sheer fatigue, trainees are yelled at—in fact, taunted—throughout the process. With expletive-laced tirades they are offered incentives to quit. And more than 70 percent do just that. A large bell hangs prominently at this Special Warfare Center. And regardless of who rings it and whatever time it's rung, the sound signals that a SEAL trainee has quit. For that individual the almost insane training is over. His helmet is removed and placed on the ground beneath the bell. He has declared publicly that becoming a Navy SEAL simply isn't worth it. He's chosen to remain an ordinary soldier rather than to endure the rigor, discipline, and mental anguish needed to join the elite ranks of the Navy SEALS.

DON'T QUIT!

In Luke 18:1 Jesus taught His twelve recruits "that they should always pray and not give up." Jesus's message is: "Don't quit! Don't ring the bell!" His counsel is followed by a parable of a persistent widow who illustrates the value of a prayer-filled lifestyle.

This widow sought justice through the local judge. Because the judge was corrupt, he refused to grant her justice though she appeared before him several times. The judge's disregard for victims like this widow was further compromised by his irreverence of the Lord. But the widow was unmoved by the judge's lack of compassion and his penchant for bribes. Her persistence resulted in a favorable ruling. The judge grew sick and tired of her repeated requests for justice (vv. 4–6). It was purely her unmitigated persistence that had worn him down.

> **God *expects* us to cry out to Him day and night. God won't ignore our pleas for justice.**

The parable of the persistent widow reinforces our call to vigilance and persistence in prayer. Although she didn't receive her answer the first time she asked, the widow ultimately gained the justice she sought through her persistence. And she symbolizes Jesus's message to us, "Don't quit! Don't ring the bell!", even in the face of delay and hardship.

The parable ends with this statement: "And will not God bring about justice for his chosen ones, who cry out to him day and night? Will he keep putting them off? I tell you, he will see that they get justice, and quickly" (vv. 7–8). God expects us to cry out to Him day and night. Unlike the unjust judge, God won't ignore our pleas for justice.

Discouragement and Prayerlessness

A deficiency of persistence and vitality in your prayer life could mean that you've become discouraged. The silent cry of many is, "Why hasn't God answered my prayers? Why is He silent toward me?" Discouraged believers often retreat to a life of spiritual apathy. They "ring the bell," abandoning the call for spiritual warfare, and their helmets of fervent prayer hit the ground with a disappointed thud. This can happen to anyone who remains unaware of Satan's skill and tactics in his use of the weapon of discouragement.

Thankfully you can combat this kind of discouragement. Too often many solid believers quit praying and abandon the call to spiritual warfare, leaving the responsibility of being kneeling warriors to others. Quitting has become far too commonplace in our generation, and when we do pray, much of our praying reflects a preoccupation with our own lives.

Kneeling warriors are charged with the task of seeking the betterment and expansion of the kingdom of God. Kneeling warriors look at the future of Christianity and not just to their own future. Kneeling warriors are preoccupied with the moral fabric of society and how to communicate a biblical worldview to our fallen culture. Similar to the kind of fighting Navy SEALS have pledged to perform, our prayers must include praying for the wide-scale openness of people toward the gospel of Jesus Christ. With this level of responsibility resting squarely on our shoulders, we can't afford to ring the bell in prayer. We must keenly understand how to engage in spiritual warfare so that the worldviews, philosophies, and diabolic teachings of the Osama bin Ladens and other societal despots of our era can be annihilated. Prayers that reflect true spiritual warfare must be strategic and powerful so that the world's evil is overshadowed by God's amazing grace.

Another key responsibility of kneeling warriors is to motivate and encourage delinquent intercessors to return to their posts of prayer. The word *intercessor* is the Hebrew word *paga* (pronounced *paw-gah*) and it means meet (together), come between, cause to entreat, and reach. It captures the function and behavior of an intermediary, an advocate, or a representative. When associated with prayer, it means an intermediary, an advocate, or a representative who brings the people's case to God in prayer. Effectiveness in this area requires that we discover why people typically drop out in the first place.

WHY PEOPLE RING THE BELL

Regardless of your age, gender, ethnicity, or national origin, the law of gravity dictates that you will come crashing to the ground at the rate of 32.2 feet per second if you jump off the roof of a building.[1] This law is both constant and nonnegotiable. In the same way there are laws associated with prayer that are constant and nonnegotiable.

> **Prayers that reflect true spiritual warfare must be strategic and powerful so that the world's evil is overshadowed by God's amazing grace.**

So what's the reason so many believers ring the bell? Simple: they don't understand the laws of prayer. We can't blame God. He clearly stated, "The prayer of the upright pleases him" (Prov. 15:8). God's power matches the generosity of His heart. It is a fundamental teaching of the Bible that God is omnipotent—all powerful. And while God loves us and wants our best, He cannot ignore His own laws of prayer.

The widow woman knew that her persistence meant she'd have to "ask." And she repeatedly asked the judge for justice. Jesus underscored this when He said, "They should always pray and not give up" (Luke 18:1). With this thought in mind Martin Luther said, "When I get hold of a promise...I look upon as I would a fruit tree....If I would get them I must shake the tree to and fro."[2]

God wants us to make requests because He delights in answering us. We ought to persistently pursue Him for all His promises because this pleases Him.

There are four common reasons for unanswered prayers:

1. The prayer may reflect wrong motives and dishonest motivations.

2. The prayer may be outside of God's will.

3. The prayer is not followed up with action.

4. The person praying may doubt God's ability or willingness to answer the prayer.

For example, if you're praying for a new job, it's important to explore whether you want the job only to get wealthy or because it's part of the will of God for your life. Are you praying for a new job but not taking the appropriate actions of preparing your résumé and consistently searching the online job boards and other sources? And because it's taking longer than anticipated for you to land a job, are you doubtful of God's willingness to answer your prayer? Avoiding these four pitfalls will naturally lead you back to a life of prayer. Unlike the Navy SEALS, in the kingdom of God you can rejoin the ranks of the kneeling warriors by picking up your helmet and placing it back on your head at any given moment. And soldier, that's exactly what you should do.

Unanswered Prayers Stem From Wrong Motives

Motives are critical in the eyes of the Lord. James—the apostle who allegedly died with camel-like knees because of his life of prayer—wrote: "You do not have, because you do not ask God. When you ask, you do not receive, because you ask with wrong motives, that you may spend what you get on your pleasures" (James 4:2–3). The principle James teaches us is this: effective prayer requires that the one praying have right motives.

The widow's moral rightness and need for justice propelled her to maintain an attitude of persistence. Her motive for justice was pure, sincere, and God honoring. Thus this point on the four-point checklist of the reasons for unanswered prayers can be crossed off.

> **Effective prayer requires that the one praying have right motives.**

In his book *God Has a Dream* Archbishop Desmond Tutu writes:

> During the darkest days of apartheid I used to say to P. W. Botha, the president of South Africa, that we had already won, and I invited him and other white South Africans to join the winning side. All the "objective" facts were against us—the past laws,

the imprisonments, the teargassing, the massacres, the murder of political activists—but my confidence was not in the present circumstances but in the laws of God's universe. This is a *moral* universe, which means that, despite all the evidence that seems to be to the contrary, there is no way that evil and injustice and oppression and lies can have the last word. God is a God who cares about right and wrong.[3]

Archbishop Tutu's revelation that God had ordered the universe on a moral axis encouraged him and other South Africans to maintain vigilance in their prayers and pursuit of justice. Their cries didn't go unheard. Apartheid was legislatively and morally overturned as being inhumane.

This law of prayer forces us to mature spiritually so we don't view God as some sort of sugar daddy whose obligation is to bring to us everything we ask Him for. Our motivation must be inspected and found righteous for our prayers to be answered by the Lord.

God gets no glory from unanswered prayers.

Evaluating your motives requires both skill and honesty. Motives are made up of passions, lusts, and unmet desires. While these things often appear to be very innocent on the surface, when held up to the light of sacred Scriptures they may turn out to be nothing more than mere fantasies. To determine whether your passion is improper, ask yourself some of the following tough questions:

- If I receive my prayer request, will I freely share the blessings with others?

- Will the kingdom of God benefit by my answered prayer?

- Will this answered prayer bring me closer to God or distance me from Him?

- Why have I been praying for these items?

- What am I really seeking?

These soul-searching questions help clarify our motives so that this law of prayer is not violated. A wrong motive points to some deficit in our lives that must be addressed. If left unchecked, the problem will creep into other areas, rendering us spiritually unhealthy. The flip side of the equation is equally meaningful. Once our motives are aligned with God's standards, the answers to our prayers are sure to be released. Remember, God gets no glory from unanswered prayers. Our willingness to please Him and to glorify His name increases exponentially as our prayers are answered. God is not more deserving of our praise when our prayers are answered. Rather, the reality is that we have become more aligned with Him in our motivation. Thus we praise Him all the more. Seek to have godly motives like the persistent widow, and God will answer your prayers.

UNANSWERED PRAYERS COME FROM
BEING OUT OF THE WILL OF GOD

During my pre-Christ days I knew firsthand what it was like to live outside of God's will, and it wasn't a pretty sight. It was a self-centered life of pain, hardship, confusion, and uncertainty. On the contrary, the will of God is a life of comfort, satisfaction, and certainty. I don't mean to imply that living within the will of God means I don't have a care in the world. Certainly there are challenges I still have to navigate. But when you are in the will of God, you experience peace that passes all understanding. You also enjoy the certainty that "in all things God works for the good of those who love him, who have been called according to his purpose" (Rom. 8:28), no matter what hardships come your way.

One of the ways God protects us from ourselves is by not answering all our prayers. He doesn't answer prayers that lead us away from His will. The Bible teaches, "This is the confidence we have in approaching God: that if we ask anything according to his will, he hears us. And if we know that he hears us—whatever we ask—we know that we have what we asked of him" (1 John 5:14–15). Prayer is a gift from God. Our prayer requests should flow out of a desire to maintain a healthy and vibrant relationship with Him. We don't want our hearts to be cold and disconnected from God, and God doesn't want us to live outside of fellowship with Him. God's will guarantees a healthy relationship with Him. To protect us from venturing outside of His will, God established this law of prayer: "I cannot answer prayers designed to take you out of My will."

The will of God reflects His desire, intent, plan, and

purpose for our lives. Being a servant of the Lord makes living in His will of paramount importance. Living in the will of God also offers a sense of security that produces confidence in our ability to approach God in prayer. This is the crux of the apostle John's statement about having confidence in prayer: requesting things in the will of God gives you confidence in receiving an audience with God and getting your request granted. Valuing the will of God means that pleasing Him is so important to you that you desire nothing outside of His will. Your relationship with God is so sacred to you that your longings, aspirations, and desires can all be met within the will of God. Your heart finds its rest in the will of God. Based on this assurance, your confidence to make requests in prayer remains constantly high. You know that you please God, and you know that your requests please God. The beautiful thing is He knows it too.

One of the ways God protects us from ourselves is by *not* answering all our prayers.

The persistent widow had confidence and peace knowing her request was in keeping with the will of God. God is always pro-justice, and He's always anti-injustice. There was no violation on her part regarding this law of prayer. She was on point.

Don't despair if your prayers are not being answered. Instead, examine your request to determine whether it's in keeping with the will of God. If it isn't, abandon the request. What joy can you derive from having your prayers answered if the result leads you away from God's will anyway? A bona fide warrior wants to serve the purpose of his commanding officer and country. In our case the purpose of our commander—the Lord Jesus—is that we live in the center of His will.

Unanswered Prayers Come When We Don't Take Action

The persistent widow never allowed discouragement to stop her from taking action. After each rejection from the judge she walked through the village to return home. You can imagine life in small Middle Eastern villages, where conversations with neighbors are unavoidable. How many times did she have to recount the judge's unwillingness to grant her justice? Although Scripture is silent on this particular point, it is clear that she was unmoved by the judge's uncaring attitude or the snickering of her neighbors for that matter. She likely had to encourage herself again and again before walking back to the courthouse each time in pursuit of justice. But this persistent widow understood that taking action is one of the laws of prayer.

Prayer gives us the wisdom to know how to move forward and what to say when the occurrence we have been praying for arrives.

Many people pray, but few take action. It's as if we view taking action as somehow theologically inappropriate. Nothing could be further from the truth. The widow knew that any justice she gained apart from the judge's ruling would be unofficial and could not be defended. The judge had to render a ruling, and securing justice would have been impossible if she had simply stayed home and prayed for it.

God uses two things to get people to act—truth and prayer. Our responsibility is to pray for the circumstances and the people involved in the situation. Prayer gives us the wisdom to know how to move forward and what to say when the occurrence we have been praying for arrives. Truth is the information used to engage the mind and to stir the heart. Praying about the spiritual state of your loved ones is a good thing. It's definitely God's will that they come to a saving knowledge of the Lord Jesus Christ, but prayer in and of itself is not going to save them. Prayer will soften your heart toward them. Prayer will soften their hearts toward the gospel. Prayer will create the needed circumstances and mind-set that welcome the gospel message. But at some point the truth of the gospel must be presented so that a decision can be reached. God has wired human beings to be moved by truth. That's why Paul declared, "I am not ashamed of the gospel, because it is the power of God for the salvation of everyone who believes" (Rom. 1:16). The believing phase follows the hearing phase. Before one can believe, he must have heard the truth of the gospel. Prayer and truth go hand in hand to yield changed lives.

Similarly prayer and action go hand in hand. The persistent widow both prayed *and* acted. Many people ring the bell and enter a state of prayerlessness because they've misunderstood this law of prayer. They waited for God to act after their extensive praying, assuming God would move apart from *their* action. Meanwhile God was waiting on them to act.

I heard a funny story about a guy on a deserted island that

started to slowly sink into the ocean. Desperate for his life he cried out to God, "Save me! I don't want to drown!" In a few minutes a huge steam liner came floating on the ocean. The captain saw the island sinking and heard the man crying to God for help. Over the ship's speakers he said to the man, "Don't despair; I'll send a rowboat to you." The man on the island yelled back, "Don't bother yourself; God will rescue me." Although the man's reply was strange, the captain sailed on. As the island kept sinking, the man kept praying for God's help. Shortly afterward a helicopter hovered above the island. The pilot said to the man, "I'll lower the rope for you to climb up." The man signaled to the pilot that he should not trouble himself because God would rescue him shortly. The pilot shook his head as he flew off.

Within a couple of hours the island sank and the man drowned. The next moment the man stood in front of the pearly gates of heaven with a quizzical look on his face. St. Peter asked him what was wrong. He said, "I just drowned. I don't know why God didn't answer my prayers for help." Peter responded, "God sent a steam liner and a helicopter; what more did you want? You never took action!"

Again, the prayerlessness of many well-intentioned believers is caused by discouragement—a by-product of their own lack of action. Praying does not and should not nullify your responsibility to take action. The only time you should refrain from taking action is when the Holy Spirit convicts you of impulsiveness or haste. In those instances you will sense Him tugging on your heart, telling you, "Wait! Don't do anything right now!" But if you're unsure whether these thoughts are from your own

Don't Ring the Bell!

mind or from the mind of God, take time to seek the advice of someone who's spiritually mature. A quick conversation with a more seasoned warrior can help clarify the course of action you ought to take.

God's Word is pregnant with power and every other vital ingredient needed to deliver on His promises. Our role is to trust Him when we pray.

Whatever you do, prayerlessness should not be the end result. If you've violated the law of prayer by not taking action, ask God to guide your steps as part of your aim to please Him. You'll find that taking action will prove a positive ingredient to your life of prayer.

UNANSWERED PRAYERS COME FROM DOUBTING GOD'S ABILITY

Faith is critical to achieving and maintaining a healthy spiritual life. The writer of Hebrews tells us, "Without faith it is impossible to please God" (Heb. 11:6). The converse is equally true: doubt displeases God. One of the laws of prayer is to always pose our requests in faith. The Bible puts it this way: "But when he asks, he must believe and not doubt, because he who doubts is like a wave of the sea, blown and tossed by the wind. That man should not think he will receive anything from the Lord; he is a double-minded man, unstable in all he does" (James 1:6–8). The apostle James taught that doubt is rooted in uncertainty. It signifies there's a question and indictment about God's ability. Doubt asks, "Does God have the power to grant my petition? And is God willing to grant my petition even though He has the power?"

Both questions are indictments against the nature of a loving and all-powerful God. These questions also accuse God of lying to us. God clearly tells us to call to Him, and He'll answer us (Jer. 33:3). Yet a doubtful disposition questions the truthfulness of God. It's important to remember God doesn't say anything He doesn't mean. He is the epitome of integrity and credibility. His Word is His bond. He honors every aspect of His Word. It is absolutely infallible. God's Word is pregnant with power and every other vital ingredient needed to deliver on His promises. Our role is to trust Him when we pray. Having faith in God is how we demonstrate that we trust Him.

The parable of the persistent widow is a lesson about how we should pray and never give up. She emulates what it means to have faith in God in the face of human opposition and a blatant disregard for justice. We can extract from this parable that the widow was not merely praying mechanical prayers—those bereft of the true sentiment of heart and a genuine embrace of God's will, leaving one deprived of the fruitfulness of a Spirit-directed life. Mechanical prayers are stiff and stilted and don't produce the answers you desire from the Lord. Faith in God, on the other hand, is fluid. It calls for an ongoing emotional and spiritual engagement. You must decide to believe God. You must intentionally choose to trust in God's promises...today.

The Navy SEAL trainees who ring the bell and give up will never know the joy of heroism. The burning desire they once had to become SEALS has been quenched by the rigor of the program. Don't let this happen to you on your way to becoming a kneeling warrior. Keep a watchful eye on the four common causes for discouragement and prayerlessness to avoid a similar outcome.

**Don't allow the words of Jesus to
fall to the earth without bearing
fruit. Pray without giving up.**

The laws of prayer can be learned. And once you have mastered them, you will invariably begin to grow in the power of prayer. You will also likely find yourself coming alongside discouraged believers to help them discover the reasons their prayers haven't been answered. You will be able to assist them in picking up their helmets, wiping the discouragement from their minds, and rejoining the ranks of the kneeling warriors.

Don't allow the words of Jesus to fall to the earth without bearing fruit. Pray without giving up. By keeping this command, the joy of obedience will be yours, and the mystery surrounding prayer will be unveiled to you since God delights in answering prayers. This is the command of our General: "Don't ring the bell!"

During World War II Japanese Lieutenant Hiroo Onoda was sent in 1944 to a remote island in the Philippines. His orders were to do all he could to hamper enemy attacks on the island. He joined forces with a group of soldiers already stationed there, but within a month all but four of the men were killed in battle. Onoda and the others took to the hills.

In 1945 they began seeing pamphlets stating the war had ended, but Onoda dismissed them as propaganda. In the following few years the others surrendered or died one by one, but Onoda held his position and even continued his guerilla activities until 1974—twenty-nine years later. Onoda finally met a college dropout named Suzuki backpacking in the island who explained to him the war had ended almost thirty years ago. The dedicated soldier was still reluctant to believe. Finally his former commanding officer, long since retired, flew to the island and gave Onoda his orders to lay down his arms.[4]

Like Lieutenant Onoda, we must learn how to keep fighting until our commanding officer, Jesus Christ, tells us to lay down our arms. Don't ring the bell until you hear Jesus's command to lay down your arms and cease praying!

Chapter 3

THE WARRIOR'S LIFE

I WAS STILL PRETTY YOUNG AND VERY INEXPERIENCED IN pastoral ministry when I was invited to speak at a conference alongside a number of spiritual giants. As a thirty-two-year-old I was acutely aware of my immaturity among these well-known preachers, but I accepted the invitation in the hopes that my small contribution would help at least someone in attendance. On the second morning of the conference I decided to attend preservice prayer. To my surprise one of the other guest speakers—a seasoned and gifted preacher—had also come to the prayer meeting. Everyone at the early morning meeting had come for the same reason—to seek the Lord.

As I watched the older preacher, I wondered, "What does a guy like that pray about after fifty fruitful years of serving God?" I felt like a baby compared to this legend, so I scooted close to him when the time came for us to kneel at the altar. I wanted to hear the prayer request of this silver-haired saint. My ears perked up as I heard him pray, "Lord, help me to walk with You in integrity and childlikeness. Help me to develop a life of prayer that reflects a genuine value of what Jesus did for me on the cross."

I couldn't help but wonder if this was the kind of prayer I'd be praying after fifty years of walking with the Lord. I was preoccupied by this question for the rest of the conference. Eventually I concluded that the lifestyle of a kneeling warrior is based on living in a state of battle readiness. The old veteran's youthful prayer gave me a glimpse that he was still excitedly fighting the good fight of faith. And that became my new life's goal—just as it was for the spiritual legend I had eavesdropped on. The simplicity of his prayer showed that his relationship with Jesus was still vibrant and that he was still in awe of the Savior. This childlike simplicity and respect for the lordship of Jesus Christ is central to the kneeling warrior's ability to maintain a state of battle readiness. The call to spiritual warfare begins there.

THE CALL TO PRAYER

Something erupted in the life of the unnamed disciple as he watched Jesus pray. Scripture describes the scene this way: "One day Jesus was praying in a certain place. When he finished, one of his disciples said to him, 'Lord, teach us to pray, just as John taught his disciples'" (Luke 11:1). What did this disciple witness? Was he struck by the intimate connection between Jesus and God the Father? Was it the unbridled joy emanating from Jesus as He communed with God? Was it the certainty that God would answer all of Jesus's requests? Regardless of whatever it was that captured this disciple's attention, it's important to note he acknowledged that he too could have that kind of rapport with the Father if he knew how to pray.

Childlike simplicity and respect for the lordship of Jesus Christ is central to the kneeling warrior's ability to maintain a state of battle readiness.

After a lesson I was teaching my congregation one night about how prayer is a two-way street—we speak and then quietly listen for God's reply—one of the ladies, Ylonda, excitedly shared this story with me.

> Years ago my best friend's then-four-year-old son was hospitalized and on the brink of death from a brain disease. It was akin to encephalitis, but wasn't. Vanessa was very active in her church and, as you can imagine, had tons of visitors coming to pray with her at the hospital. Some days I watched folks stand with Vanessa at her son's bedside praying for hours, but once they got out of her earshot, some of these folks—all of whom I considered really strong spiritual leaders—would break down and cry with hopelessness.

One day, after witnessing another round of folks coming and going from the boy's room, I went to sit with Vanessa. She was looking at her son, Caleb, stroking his hand and smiling with real joy. Now, without being too graphic, to me that baby looked like one of the third-world kids you see on those Save the Children commercials. His body was emaciated, and he couldn't close his mouth, so his lips were dry and cracked. Mind you, just weeks prior he'd been out riding his bike and being as rambunctious and as outgoing as any other little boy. I reached to hug Vanessa, and she was still smiling brightly. Then she whispered to me, "God is good; look how handsome Caleb looks today." And then she kept saying over and over, "Thank You, God, for my baby's healing." I thought then and there—some ten years ago—I want to know prayer like that. For months doctor after doctor came in to deliver one discouraging prognosis after another, and Vanessa would smile and say, "You think so, huh?"

Years later when we talked about Caleb's recovery, I asked her about those episodes. Vanessa simply said, "Those doctors couldn't hear what God was telling me."

Ylonda's point underscored exactly what I had been teaching: prayer requires listening just as much as speaking, if not more. We must wait to hear what God has to say to us about our request of Him.

The moment Jesus finished praying, the disciple blurted out his childlike request: "Teach us to pray." It took both courage and humility to admit his ignorance about prayer. It was an admission conveying his lowly position and his appropriate reverence of the Teacher's lofty stature. This unnamed disciple desperately wanted to make a real and satisfying connection with Almighty God the way he saw Jesus had, but he knew he needed to learn.

Similarly you begin answering the call to prayer by admitting that you need to learn. Saint Augustine, one of the most important figures in the ancient Western church, said, "Humility is the foundation of all the other virtues hence, in the soul in which this virtue does not exist there cannot be any other virtue except in mere appearance."[1]

HUMILITY IS THE STARTING POINT TO PRAYER

Charles Spurgeon said, "Humility is to make a right estimate of one's-self."[2] The Bible teaches that "when pride comes, then comes disgrace, but with humility comes wisdom" (Prov. 11:2). The unnamed disciple recognized his need for a solid foundation in prayer. He didn't let his pride obstruct his deep desire to connect with God. Sure, the other disciples were around, and I'm sure he felt a bit uncomfortable being so vulnerable in front of the other guys. Nonetheless, he allowed humility to open the door to a deeper experience of intimacy with God.

Similarly, if you want to become a powerful kneeling warrior, you must admit your need to learn more about prayer. No one can do it for you. As Priscilla Shirer—a Bible teacher and author—admits, "When I wasn't hearing from God...I saw that God often spoke to people because they were prepared to hear from Him, and I realized maybe He was waiting on me to position myself to hear His voice."[3] Even after reading tons of books on prayer, I've repeatedly come face-to-face with my own ignorance about the depth and breadth of this essential spiritual practice. Each step along the way has given me a deeper appreciation for the value of prayer—developing stronger passion within me to grow more astutely in the art of prayer.

Learning to pray requires that we first value prayer. Sure, becoming a student and absorbing the academic principles of prayer will give you an intellectual understanding of its principles. But connecting with God in a deep and meaningful way begins with meekness and your sincere appreciation of the spiritual intimacy you can have with God.

In his classic book *The Pursuit of God* A. W. Tozer wrote: "Come near to the holy men and women of the past and you will soon feel the heat of their desire after God. They mourned for Him, they prayed and wrestled and sought for Him day and night, in season and out, and when they had found Him the finding was all the sweeter for the long seeking."[4] These historic believers learned that real praying begins with a quest for a healthy and vibrant relationship with God.

BE CONFIDENT IN GOD

God genuinely cares for our welfare. Prayer begins when we approach Him with boldness—reflecting the fact that we feel welcome to approach Him. This frank approach does not imply irreverence toward God, however. Because we are in relationship with God, we have the right to make a logical assumption that God already knows us and we already know Him. So formality and putting on airs in prayer is totally inappropriate. Prayer invites you to approach God the way you would a close, albeit all-powerful, friend who is comfortable with your direct speech and attitude.

On one occasion when Jesus boldly prayed at the graveside of Lazarus, His confidence in God's attentiveness to His prayers preceded His requests: "Father, I thank you that you have heard me. I knew that you always hear me" (John 11:41–42). We too are urged to cultivate this level of confidence in God before we pray. The writer of Hebrews said, "Let us then approach the throne of grace with *confidence*, so that we may receive mercy and find grace to help us in our time of need" (Heb. 4:16, emphasis added).

> **Prayer begins when we approach Him
> with boldness—reflecting the fact that
> we feel welcome to approach Him.**

Effective prayer comes from having confidence in approaching God. John wrote, "This is the confidence we have in approaching God: that if we ask anything according to his will, he hears us. And if we know that he hears us—whatever we ask—we know that we have what we asked of him" (1 John 5:14–15). Where does such confidence come from? This level of certainty requires your total vulnerability before God. You must willingly allow Him to search your life and guide you toward the right moral, ethical, and logistical track. You must also give Him the freedom to shepherd you the way He deems appropriate. And you must wholeheartedly embrace His guidance, correction, and love.

Our confidence in approaching God also comes from knowing that His throne is one of *mercy* and *grace*. Mercy conveys a sympathetic understanding of the frailty of humankind. This is why Hebrews 4:15 says, "For we do not have a high priest who is unable to sympathize with our weaknesses, but we have one who has been tempted in every way, just as we are—yet without sin." God understands humanity's need for help even though Christ—God in flesh—never sinned. The confidence we have in approaching God originates from understanding that He will never condemn us. We can approach Him boldly because He understands *how* and *why* we need His help.

Grace communicates God's willingness to empower us with the ability to both *do* and to *be* whatever He has assigned for us. Grace extends power through the Holy Spirit to see that God's intention is carried out in us. This generous reality about God's throne makes appearing before Him with confidence inviting. God's sole intention is to improve and strengthen our lives. And even when we sin, His motive is not to hurt or get even with us. Instead God extends His grace to help us achieve satisfying lives. The eminent Greek scholar Kenneth Wuest said this about grace:

> The word "grace" is one of the most precious words In Scripture. Archbishop Trench in his *Synonyms of the New Testament* says of this word in the Greek language, "It is hardly too much to say that the Greek mind has in no word uttered itself and all that was in its heart more distinctly than in

this." The Greeks were lovers of beauty, in nature, in their architecture, their statuary, their poetry, their drama. Anything which called out the heart wonder, admiration, pleasure, or joy, was designated by this word. The word came to signify the doing of a favor graciously, spontaneously, a favor done without expectation of return but arising only out of the generosity of the giver.[5]

Given this beautiful description of grace, confidence in prayer is easy. Any anxiety you may have had regarding approaching God can be dispelled because His grace welcomes you with open arms.

**Grace extends power through the Holy Spirit
to see that God's intention is carried out in us.**

You Can Learn How to Pray

The unnamed disciple's request suggests we *can* learn to pray. He pointed it out this way: "John [the Baptist] taught his disciples" how to pray (Luke 11:1). The disciple's request also suggests that prayer can be taught. He wasn't referring to rote or formulaic praying. The disciple was referring to real, heartfelt praying that flows out of a genuine connection with God. Yes, even this kind of praying can be learned.

According to E. M. Bounds, the twentieth-century kneeling warrior, "Prayer is a trade to be learned, and it is a life trade. We must be apprentices and serve our time at it. Painstaking care, much thought, practice and labor are required to be a skillful tradesman in praying."[6] In other words, we learn by doing. You learn how to pray by praying just as you can only learn how to swim by...swimming.

Before you become skilled in prayer, you have to immerse yourself in the practice of praying. Jesus answered the disciple by saying: "When you pray, say..." (Luke 11:2). He commences to outline one of the most famous prayers—the Lord's Prayer. The point I'm making is Jesus taught that the way you learn how to pray is by praying. Thus we can deduce the skill of prayer is learned as you yield to the discipline of prayer.

C. H. Spurgeon in his book *Lectures to My Students* instructed young preachers about the need to develop a private life of prayer. He drew an illustration from one of his contemporaries, Joseph Alleine, an English Puritan pastor and author of many books, by saying, "'At the time of his health,' writes his wife, 'he did rise constantly at or before four of the clock, and would be much troubled if he heard smiths or other craftsmen at their trades before he was at communion with God; saying to me often, "How this noise shames me. Does not my Master deserve more than theirs?" From four till eight he spent in prayer, holy contemplation, and singing psalms, in which he much delighted and did daily practice alone, as well as in the family.'"[7]

SET A TIME OF PRAYER

Daniel the prophet and statesman modeled a disciplined life of prayer. Scripture teaches that, "Three times a day he got down on his knees and prayed, giving thanks to his God" (Dan. 6:10).

Like many people I used to feel as though I had no time to pray regularly. I hid behind such excuses as: I don't have time. I have to take care of my children. I have to go to work. I have to cook, clean the house, grocery shop, and any other distraction I could come up with. All these excuses justified my undisciplined prayer life. I once read, "Those who use the 'too busy syndrome,' their prayerless souls have developed an immunity to prayer." Powerful! I wish I had said that! Seems I just did.

Establishing a set time of prayer occurs only when you intentionally designate a specific time in your daily calendar as "prayer time." As a prime minister in Babylon Daniel was quite busy tending to governmental affairs, yet he took time to develop and guard his life of prayer (Dan. 2:48; 5:29). Setting a time of prayer requires that you understand how your biological clock works. If you are a morning person, set a prayer time in the morning. If you are a night owl, choose a time at night when you can give yourself to uninterrupted prayer. In his classic book *Prayer* Professor Hallesby states: "The first and the decisive battle in connection with prayer is the conflict which arises when we are to make arrangements to be alone with God every day."[8]

> **Those who use the "too busy syndrome," their prayerless souls have developed an immunity to prayer.**

My prayer time is in the morning between 4:00 and 5:00 a.m. That's when everyone in my home is asleep and there is no interruption. I've always been a morning person. In fact, when I got married some thirty years ago, Marlinda would complain when I'd try to engage her in deep conversations at 4:00 a.m. "Only someone insane is this happy and bubbly so early in the morning," she would often say. I shrugged it off and kept talking until she'd fall back to sleep. My prayer partner is also a morning person, and we pray by phone every Wednesday morning at 4:30 a.m. It's our best hour of the week.

If your life is so unpredictable you cannot set a daily time of prayer, something is drastically wrong. The enemy of your soul has a major foothold in your life. C. S. Lewis writes in *The Screwtape Letters* of how Screwtape (a demon in higher echelons of hellish status) trains his nephew Wormwood (a lower-ranking demon) to distract believers from prayer by interfering at any price in any fashion when people start to pray. The allegory makes this point clear from the enemy's perspective: *real prayer is lethal* to their cause.[9] Even in our contemporary era this allegory still proves true. The enemy of our souls continues to trick people with excuses. Perhaps Screwtape and Wormwood are hindering your ability to carve out a set time of prayer. Remember, the pursuit of God must become a daily one. Your thirst to know God and to be used of Him cannot be periodic or random. God deserves better, and you have the ability to live up to His expectations. Set a time of prayer!

Only a dire emergency should interrupt your time of prayer—and only when it's a legitimate emergency. If you allow life's typical mishaps to creep into this time, causing disruptions in your prayer schedule, you will slowly get pulled back into a lifestyle of prayerlessness despite your best intentions.

SET A PLACE OF PRAYER

Daniel was determined to live the life of a kneeling warrior. This became possible because he *set a place of prayer*. Scripture depicts his place of prayer this way: "He went home to his upstairs room where the windows opened toward Jerusalem. Three times a day he got down on his knees and prayed, giving thanks to his God" (Dan. 6:10). Daniel had discovered a secret to a disciplined life of prayer—a regular place to meet with God. In Daniel's case it was an upstairs room in his home where he could look out toward Jerusalem—the holy and sacred city of the Hebrew people.

> **Your thirst to know God and to be**
> **used of Him cannot be periodic or**
> **random. God deserves better.**

Like every other intercessor Daniel exercised his freedom to pray not only in his set place but also anywhere—even in the lions' den (v. 22). Prayer must have been a regular part of his spiritual strength and knack for dream interpretation during his early days in Babylon when he and his three friends—Hananiah, Mishael, and Azariah—underwent a rigorous orientation to Babylonian culture (Dan. 1:11–16). Daniel must have understood David's song in Psalm 139:7–10, which reads:

> Where can I go from your Spirit?
>   Where can I flee from your presence?
> If I go to the heavens, you are there;
>   if I make my bed in the depths, you are there.

If I rise on the wings of the dawn,
  if I settle on the far side of the sea,
even there your hand will guide me,
  your right hand will hold me fast.

My set place of prayer is my home office. One day while I was working there, Marlinda came in and pointed to one of the chairs. "That must be your place of prayer," she said. "How do you know?" I asked. "The oil from your hair left a stain on that particular spot of the chair. That's where you lay your head as you pray." Duly embarrassed, I nodded my head in agreement.

Setting a defined place of prayer helps minimize distractions as you intercede. If you're anything like me, distractions can take you completely off track. For instance, I can walk into a room and notice a crooked picture on the wall. I *have* to straighten it—even if it's not in my house. I find it tough to concentrate on the task at hand unless things around me are in order. It's almost impossible for me to pray in a room that's in disarray. Instead of focusing on prayer, I become preoccupied with tidying up the room. But even with my own idiosyncrasies I continue to uphold a no-excuses policy when it comes to prayer.

Lots of people probably say, "My ideal prayer space is often cluttered." Perhaps you should clear a space on a desk or kitchen table or create a makeshift prayer spot. Or maybe you can alter your tolerance for clutter. One lady did just that. After her third child came along, she almost never found a place where there wasn't a toy soldier or a LEGO piece. So she began to look at the "mess" as a sign of God's loving grace—focusing on the idea of having been blessed with a healthy baby boy and an active family.

I've heard people use other excuses like, "I live in a small apartment, and there's no suitable space for prayer." I ask, "What about your bedroom?" And if that doesn't work I ask, "What about the bathroom?" If they rule that out too, I go even further, asking, "What about your closet?" The point is, all you need is a small amount of space where you can be uninterrupted and focused on pursuing the Lord in prayer.

If you are going to enter the ranks of the kneeling warriors, you must establish a set place of prayer.

Dick Eastman in his book *The Hour That Changes the World* wrote: "Consider Susanna Wesley. The mother of nineteen children, including John and Charles [founders of the Methodist Church], Susanna Wesley still found time to pray daily. This godly saint seldom gave the Lord less than a full hour each day for prayer.... Susanna Wesley...had no specific place for prayer. So, at her chosen time for spiritual exercise she would take her apron and pull it over her face. Her children were instructed never to disturb 'mother' when she was praying in her apron."[10] While this may sound over the top to you, consider how her two sons have helped shape the world. Placing an apron over her head was a very small price to pay for such awesome results.

If you are going to enter the ranks of the kneeling warriors, you must establish a set place of prayer. Don't put it off until you get a bigger home or the kids go off to college. Today is the day of decision, but you're not stuck with your decision. You can always change your prayer space next month, next year, or whenever the need arises. The point is, you must set a place of prayer right now.

SET AN AGENDA OF PRAYER

Drawing wisdom once again from the life of Daniel, we learn he had a set time of prayer, a set place of prayer, and *a set agenda of prayer* (Dan. 6:10). A prayer agenda is a list of things you want to cover in your appointment with God. Just as great meetings have specific agenda items, great times of prayer have agenda items too. Daniel's agenda items included things like giving thanks to God, meeting the needs of Jerusalem, seizing the promises of God for that holy city and its people, and seeking God's help regarding his personal life (v. 11).

Although we can only speculate on the other items on Daniel's prayer agenda, we can be certain he was not self-absorbed during his prayer time. Kneeling warriors have been commissioned by God to build and expand the kingdom of God, to safeguard the saints, and to win the lost by praying powerfully. These things can only be achieved when you take a strategic approach to praying.

Whenever I teach on the topic of how to set an agenda of prayer, I always draw a circle and break it into five parts. Each part represents a substantive area of spiritual responsibility that kneeling warriors must assume is part of their prayer focus. I label each of the five spaces with one of five Ps to create a prayer agenda. (See "Prayer Chart.") The five Ps are passions, people, possessions, purpose, and problems. I instruct students to allot six minutes per area to cover a broad spectrum of the concerns of the person they're praying for in just thirty minutes. The meaning of each "P" can be changed if you are praying for organizations, nations, generational groups, or anything that has become a burden of your heart.

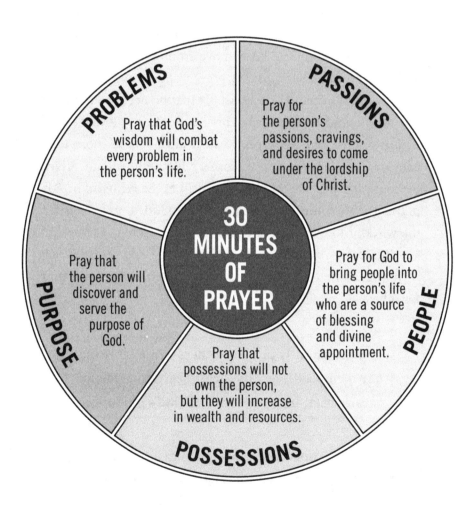

This grid is a useful guide for structuring the various areas you are praying about beyond the areas of your own life. For example, if I wanted to pray for my brother who lives with his family in Maryland, I would use this prayer guide. I would pray, "God, help Norman to control his *passions* so that they don't bring him outside of Your will. Give him passion for his wife, Althea, and their son, Kyle. Surround them with *people* who love and care for them deeply. Provide them with the *people* who have gifts and skills in areas they lack so that their lives will be full and complete." As I move around the circle, I would get to the word *possessions*. My prayer would continue as I ask God to give Norman the *possessions* that he needs to live a satisfying life and to effectively run his business. "Provide him with property and resources so he'll always have more than enough. And Lord, may my brother's life be filled and driven by Your *purpose*; one that has Your will at the center of it." My prayer then culminates with my asking God to give Norman the wisdom to overcome the *problems* he's facing. As you can see, this prayer guide is quite simple to use and provides you with a focus that allows you to be thorough in how you pray for others.

If we constantly pray for others while ignoring our own needs, our lives will begin to evidence cracks that indicate a lack of God's guidance.

Some intercessors create prayer lists that include the names of people they are moved by the Holy Spirit to pray for. You can also expand these lists to include nations, societal issues, and the unfulfilled promises God has impressed upon your heart.

The point of creating this kind of agenda is to ensure that the biblical requirement "that requests, prayers, intercession and thanksgiving be made for everyone—for kings and all those in authority, that we may live peaceful and quiet lives in all godliness and holiness" (1 Tim. 2:1–2) is met when you enter your place of prayer. An agenda also helps you to create a prayer shield around the major areas of your life and family. If we constantly pray for others while ignoring our own needs, our lives will begin to evidence cracks that indicate a lack of God's guidance. Taking on a holistic approach to prayer helps us to maintain a warrior's perspective of spiritual vigilance.

Living the life of a kneeling warrior takes commitment and constant readiness. And, like Daniel, you must maintain a posture of readiness at all times. His set place of prayer was never ignored because he developed the habit of prayer. If prayer is not your first love, make it your first discipline, and you too will become a kneeling warrior.

PART TWO

ENGAGE YOUR FAITH

Chapter 4

THE WEAPONS OF A
KNEELING WARRIOR

N O ONE WOULD CALL FORMER US SECRETARY OF State General Colin Powell a slacker. The first and only African American to serve on the Joint Chiefs of Staff is an American statesman and four-star general. Yet, by his own admission, he was "unprecocious and unaccomplished"[1] in his youth. In fact, his inability to stick to anything along with his C average in school was a great source of concern for his parents, Jamaican immigrants who stressed academic excellence and personal achievement.

Then something changed all that. He joined the military. "I had found something that I did well. I could lead. The discovery was no small gift for a young man at age twenty."[2]

A sharp and drastic change comes over a person who trades civilian life for that of a soldier. A similar change occurs when you change your status from that of a spiritual civilian to a kneeling warrior. A host of benefits emerge when you become serious about prayer—just like joining the military. The military instills purpose, productivity, and goals into the lives of newly enlisted men and women. And these qualities result in their gaining disciplined lives.

Before you can be trained in the art of spiritual warfare and become familiar with the weapons God has entrusted to us, you must recognize that your life will never be the same. In fact, it would be dangerous for you and the soldiers who serve alongside you to hold on to a civilian's mind-set. The United States military structure features four distinct categories: civilians, Army Reserves, National Guard, and military personnel. The responses of those within each category would be quite different should a war break out.

Civilians are not enlisted in the war, nor have they been trained in warfare tactics or combat techniques. They are spectators and not direct participants. Civilians have no official government mandate to bear arms in the event of war. They are ordinary people who enjoy the freedoms afforded by the military.

Army Reserves are citizens who have been officially inducted into the army and receive ongoing training while maintaining their civilian careers. These part-time soldiers fight only when they are officially deployed—which may or may not occur during their careers. These are not full-time combat troops. A member of the Army Reserves may work as a full-time accountant but participate in drill exercises with the Reserves one weekend a month to keep his skills sharp. And each year members of the Reserves are required to participate in rigorous field and specialty training for an additional two-week period.

Some Christians take this part-time approach to spiritual warfare. They're more preoccupied with their career or family and not primarily focused on the advancement of the kingdom of God. To these part-time warriors the rigor of military life only occurs sporadically—such as when a family crisis arises requiring heavy prayer and fasting. The comfort of civilian life is where they spend the majority of their time.

> **Enlistment into the army of God is not optional. It is a command. And God's army is a full-time one.**

The National Guard is another option for US citizens. Like the Army Reserves, these are civilians who serve on a part-time basis one weekend a month and one two-week period a year. Members of the National Guard can live and work where they choose because their primary attention is placed on their civilian lives. Unlike the Reserves, the National Guard has a dual mission—to serve both state and federal governments should a need arise. Although deployment is a possibility, these men and women primarily function as civilians with all the creature comforts afforded by civilian life.

The last category is that of full-time military soldiers. These are professional soldiers whose singular focus is on fighting. They don't have the luxury of going home after a weekend of duty or becoming physically or mentally soft between missions. The lifestyle of an active duty solider calls for constant battle readiness with an ambition to become better soldiers each year. They are not distracted by civilian activities and choices. They don't know the meaning of relaxing devoid of the thought, What happens if war breaks out today? Am I ready? This is the kind of perspective Paul held when he said to Timothy, "Endure hardship with us like a good soldier of Christ Jesus" (2 Tim. 2:3). Like Paul, Timothy was to think, function, and live like a professional soldier—a full-time kneeling warrior engaged in kingdom business.

If we pursue the spiritual ambition of becoming excellent soldiers, we can't avoid the rigors of boot camp, learning effective combat tactics and combat weapons: defensive weapons guard and protect against attacks, while the offensive weapons help soldiers advance and make progress against the enemy.

Which category best fits your lifestyle of prayer—civilian, Army Reserves, National Guard, or military? Most believers don't live like full-time spiritual soldiers. But the call to engage in spiritual warfare is being answered by more and more people each day. Believers are beginning to take seriously the command of sacred Scripture that says, "Put on the full armor of God so that you can take your stand against the devil's schemes" (Eph. 6:11). Enlistment into the army of God is not optional. It is a command. And God's army is a full-time one. We don't have the option of functioning as part-time soldiers. The stakes are too high for us to desire the rewards of trained professional soldiers while living like civilians. Let's go all the way and function like professional soldiers.

If we pursue the spiritual ambition of becoming excellent soldiers, we can't avoid the rigors of boot camp. In the US military you begin learning effective combat tactics the moment you enter boot camp. You also learn about combat weapons. These weapons, even in spiritual warfare, fall into two categories—*defensive* weapons and *offensive* weapons. The defensive weapons *guard* and *protect* against attacks, while the offensive weapons help soldiers *advance* and *make progress* against the enemy.

Learn to Use Your Defensive Weapons

In Ephesians 6 Paul lists a number of our defensive spiritual weapons. Other weapons can be found throughout the New Testament. The chart below captures the majority of our defensive weapons in one list reflecting God's concern for our effectiveness in spiritual warfare.

DEFENSIVE WEAPONS		
1	Wearing the full armor	Eph. 6:11–13
2	Standing firm against Satan *(remaining in God's will)*	Eph. 6:13–14
3	The belt of truth	Eph. 6:14
4	The breastplate of righteousness	Eph. 6:14
5	The shield of faith	Eph. 6:16
6	The helmet of salvation	Eph. 6:17
7	Prayer	Eph. 6:18
8	Practicing forgiveness	2 Cor. 2:8–11
9	Submission to God	James 4:7
10	Standing firm in the faith *(obeying God's Word)*	1 Pet. 5:9
11	Practicing self-control	1 Pet. 5:8
12	Staying alert	1 Pet. 5:8

Because Satan regularly launches attacks against us, God provides defensive weapons for our protection. Peter writes:

> Be self-controlled and alert. Your enemy the devil prowls around like a roaring lion looking for someone to devour. Resist him, standing firm in the faith, because you know that your brothers throughout the world are undergoing the same kind of sufferings.
>
> —1 PETER 5:8–9

Satan is always looking for some area of weakness to exploit and for some unprotected area of our lives he can influence.

God encourages us to use our defensive weapons and to become skilled in protecting the valuables He has entrusted to us. Let's explore the power of each defense weapon in our list.

Wearing the full armor

Becoming a kneeling warrior means you follow Paul's advice in Ephesians 6:11 to "put on the full armor of God so that you can take your stand against the devil's schemes." Putting on the armor is more than just a trial fitting. Much like the case when a person leaves civilian life and becomes a professional soldier, the full armor of God is to become your permanent uniform. It is a sign to you and to others you are on full-time spiritual warfare duty. It shows you are always ready to spring into action to fight against any of Satan's attacks. Alma, a corporate executive with a young family, suits up daily, in more ways than one. Each morning she takes an hour to pray, read the Bible, and sing along with the worship music from her iPod. Afterward Alma is confident she's clothed with her full armor and ready to take on life's challenges.

Standing firm against Satan

When you take a defensive posture, you decide, up front, that you won't retreat. Retreating would mean yielding a valued promise of God, part of your destiny, or a prized possession to the will of Satan. Paul advises us to stand firm against the tricks of Satan (Eph. 6:13–14). This defense posture of standing firm will keep you committed to the will of God no matter how difficult or uncomfortable the challenge becomes. For instance, if you believe God blessed you with your current job, why let the devil drive you away from it? Stand your ground!

Standing firm in the will of God is like a security blanket. It's one of God's most precious tools for protecting us. In Colossians 4:12 Epaphras wrestled in prayer for those at Colosse, "that you may stand firm in all the will of God, mature and fully assured" (Col. 4:12). Similarly it is my prayer that you defend yourself against the hordes of hell by standing firm in *all* the will of God.

> **Much like the case when a person leaves civilian life and becomes a professional soldier, the full armor of God is to become your permanent uniform.**

Frank, one of the members of my congregation, felt compelled to move his family to another side of town—forcing the children to change schools and uprooting their social lives. I questioned why he wanted to put them through such drastic change. Although he couldn't answer me at that moment, Frank went to prayer and discovered he was really searching to fill a void in his own life. He was bored and felt powerless against the trials related to his auto parts business. Frank was also feeling disillusioned because he was getting older. Ultimately he opted to stay put—discovering the full meaning of standing in the known will of God. I then provided some needed pastoral counsel to help him properly deal with the issues he was facing.

The belt of truth

Did you know that truth telling is a defensive weapon? Paul compared what was a familiar sight in his day—a Roman soldier's thick leather belt—to truth telling as an essential element to victory in the Christian life. The Roman soldier's belt held his sword and other equipment much the way today's infantryman's gear is held up by a strong belt. When fully equipped and fastened around a modern soldier's waist, the belt is a sign that he's ready to fight. Arming yourself with truth offers unparalleled defensive strength. Truth liberates. It frees you from the clutches of sin by protecting your integrity and credibility. Allowing truth to be your spiritually defensive stance means you have vowed to live a blameless, sincere, and circumspect life. A life defined by truth survives the tricks and assaults of the evil one.

Parenting is not an easy job. The task is further compounded when you discover you cannot preselect the type of child you want. You desire an athlete; God gives you a musician. You long for a singer; your child loves sports. Danielle, my oldest, struggled seriously with math when she was in seventh grade. I had earned a master's degree in civil engineering and worked for environmental consulting firms prior to entering the ministry, so math was an easy subject for me. Each evening I would sit with her in an attempt to help her understand the material, but the result was always the same. We'd both become frustrated with one another and tempers would flare.

While her stress stemmed from misunderstanding the material, mine came from believing that she could understand it but just wanted to be difficult. One night I was so angry the only thing I could do was go into my study, shut the door, and pray. I needed God to help her "get it." That was my thinking. She was the problem, I thought. A few minutes into praying the Holy Spirit spoke these precise words to my heart, "David, you sent her to that school!"

> **A life defined by truth survives the tricks and assaults of the evil one.**

Immediately I stopped praying. The truth spoken by the Holy Spirit liberated me. My anger vanished instantly. The mystery was solved. My children had been in a private Christian school through the sixth grade. Their new school placed a greater emphasis on math and science—the very areas in which Danielle struggled. I left my study armed with the knowledge of what I had to do: hire a tutor for Danielle and preserve our relationship. Had I not prayed, I would not have learned the truth, which helped me form the right perspective.

The breastplate of righteousness

The way today's police officers typically wear bulletproof vests to cover their vital organs from gunfire is the way a Roman soldier covered his chest and back with a breastplate in the days when Paul wrote his letter to the church at Ephesus. Paul wanted us to guard our hearts—the devil's primary target. In God's infinite wisdom He devised *righteousness* as the protective fabric of our spiritual breastplate. The moment we accepted Christ as our Savior, His righteousness was credited to us. Referring to Jesus, Paul taught, "God made him who had no sin to be sin for us, so that in him we might become the righteousness of God" (2 Cor. 5:21).

By walking in the ways of Christ, we walk in the ways of righteousness. This defensive weapon is used to ensure that our character, ethics, morals, and overall behavior reflect that of a genuine Christ-follower. Holiness is a defensive weapon.

The shield of faith

Again Paul draws a reference from the Roman soldier's armor to illustrate a spiritual truth. The Roman soldier used two types of shields. One was small and light and generally used in hand-to-hand combat. The other was a larger shield, about four feet tall by two and a half feet wide, and it was used to protect the soldier from arrows and other projectile strikes. The old saying was, "You either return from battle with your shield or on your shield."

Some have erroneously referred to the shield of faith as the body of beliefs or doctrine of a Christian, but Paul was referring to the trust and a confidence we must have in God. The defensive weapon known as the shield of faith is our trust and reliance on God for His protection and promises. The Bible declares, "He [God] is a shield for all who take refuge in him" (Ps. 18:30). The action of relying upon God quenches all the fiery darts Satan uses to have us live doubt-filled lives.

The helmet of salvation

The Roman soldier's helmet was created from thick leather often covered with metal. It protected the soldier in battle from swinging swords, flaming arrows, and piercing spears. The defensive use of the helmet of salvation is that it gives us assurance that upon conversion we have been adopted into the family of God. We belong to Him. Our problems become *His* problems. He will fight *for us*. He will fight *with us* and against our common foe, Satan. We can see that Paul viewed the helmet of salvation as priceless when he prayed, "…the eyes of your heart may be enlightened in order that you may know the hope to which he has called you, the riches of his glorious inheritance in the saints, and his incomparably great power for us who believe" (Eph. 1:18–19).

> **The defensive weapon known as the shield of faith is our trust and reliance on God for His protection and promises.**

Mike, a recovering alcoholic, confessed to me after a Sunday morning service that all week he'd been tempted to take a drink. He resisted each time by praying fervently. Perhaps, just as importantly, he learned his salvation was powerful enough to overcome the urge to drown his problems in the bottle.

Prayer

Paul writes in Ephesians 6:18, "And pray in the Spirit on all occasions with all kinds of prayers and requests. With this in mind, be alert and always keep on praying for all the Lord's people." Here we see prayer as both a defensive and offensive weapon. I will delve more into the nature of prayer as it relates to spiritual warfare in chapter 6.

Practicing forgiveness

A commitment to practice forgiveness is not simply good for you; it is a defensive weapon in spiritual warfare. Paul gave the Christians in Corinth the following insight: "I have forgiven in the sight of Christ for your sake, in order that Satan might not outwit us. For we are not unaware of his schemes" (2 Cor. 2:10–11). Paul's experience with spiritual warfare and defending himself against Satan's attacks taught him that unforgiveness gives Satan the legal right to attack. The converse then is equally true. Forgiveness takes away Satan's right to infiltrate your heart and life.

Forgiving those who have offended and hurt you is a powerfully defensive weapon. Remember the Old Testament character Joseph? Without a smidgen of anger, bitterness, or resentment against his jealous brothers who sold him into slavery, he practiced forgiveness, and it gave him access to God's promises for his life. You too can experience the blessing of unobstructed access to the promises of God by putting this defensive weapon to use.

Submission to God

Satan has no legal right to touch you if you're walking in total submission to God and His will for your life. James puts it this way: "Submit yourselves, then, to God. Resist the devil, and he will flee from you" (James 4:7). Submission means total surrender and compliance to God's desires and direction for your life. When you strap this defensive weapon to your life, there is nothing Satan can do to hurt you.

This played out for Marcus, a member of my church, when

he was presented with two job offers. He decided to go with the lower-paying job because it offered greater chances of growth and development, and the culture of the company was a better fit for his lifestyle—offering flexibility and better benefits. He shared with me, however, that what led him to choose one job over the other was the fact that he sensed the peace of God toward that particular company. Being in the will of God was more valuable to him than making a few extra dollars. Without any second-guessing, Marcus learned that submission to God is a surefire way to spiritual and natural victory.

> **Satan has no legal right to touch you if you're walking in total submission to God and His will for your life.**

Standing firm in the faith

Peter tells us that we can resist Satan and his attacks by standing firm in the faith (1 Pet. 5:9). This defensive action suggests that believing and obeying God's Word anchors us. We don't have to retreat or relinquish precious ground to the enemy. We successfully resist Satan's assaults when we allow the Bible to become the basis of our faith and life practice.

You can apply this defensive weapon in every area of your life—including your parenting. Stand firm in the faith as you raise your children in the fear of the Lord, and God will help you gain the success you desire regarding their welfare.

Practicing self-control

Peter is a biblical author who learned firsthand the pain and disappointment a lack of self-control can produce. In 1 Peter 5:8 we learn from him that self-control is a defensive weapon. Again, it reads, "Be self-controlled and alert. Your enemy the devil prowls around like a roaring lion looking for someone to devour." As you practice the ability to restrain and control your actions, feelings, and emotions, you will be able to stand your ground when the day of evil comes.

The lack of self-control is seen when a young lady becomes involved with the wrong man in the hopes of filling a void created by an unloving father. Had she exercised this defensive weapon, she would not have moved ahead of God by choosing to be with a guy who doesn't fit the Bible's standards of a marriageable man for one of God's daughters. The lack of self-control is also seen when a young man decides to jump at the higher-paying job offer rather than solicit God's guidance through prayer. This is a reflection of a lack of self-control and many other things. These types of social problems can be avoided when people practice self-control. Without it, a kneeling warrior is always needed to pray such victims to a place of emotional and spiritual health.

Staying alert

Do you remember when Jesus told Peter that Satan desired to sift him like wheat? Peter was so spiritually inept that he even tried to correct Jesus (Luke 22:31–33). It was years later that Peter admonished us about staying alert as a defensive weapon all Christ-followers must employ (1 Pet. 5:8). The caution here is that Satan is on the prowl looking for unsuspecting people whom he may devour. Staying alert means we must never underestimate our opponent. We should never minimize the impact of sin. We should never play with temptation, nor should we ever entertain the idea of living outside of the will of God. Alertness is readiness. Alertness is watchfulness—not just for ourselves but also for our brothers and sisters in the Lord and for others we deeply love.

My friend Phil shared a little story with me that highlights the importance of being spiritually alert in every area of life. His body had been feeling really weird for about a week or so. He noticed it when his body started to tingle. It began with his tongue, moved to his throat, and then to his overall body. After he felt this way for a while, the feeling would simply go away. Without knowing what to make of it, Phil started to pray. Within a few minutes the Holy Spirit spoke to his heart that his ailment was triggered by a food allergy. He began to do a little detective work writing down the foods he'd eaten several times over the past two weeks. To his pleasant surprise he discovered that he'd began eating something new—peaches. Come to find out, Phil was allergic to peaches. He stopped eating them, and the tingling sensation stopped. Staying spiritually alert is a defensive weapon that can help us in many areas of life.

LEARN TO USE
YOUR OFFENSIVE WEAPONS

Paul's instructions in Ephesians 6 were not limited to defensive weapons but included training of the Christian in the use of offensive weapons as well. Just as a natural army cannot win a war by only being good at defense, we too must become adept in using offensive weapons. These help us advance into new territories for Christ and aid us in strategizing, initiating, and launching attacks against the enemy through our authority in Christ.

Effective kneeling warriors ask such calculated military questions as: What is Satan trying to do? What areas of my life is God trying to promote? The answers result in their proactive development of spiritual actions aimed at advancing the will of God.

Take a look at the chart below, which lists some of the offensive weapons we must learn to use through the help of the Holy Spirit.

	OFFENSIVE WEAPONS	
1	Wearing the full armor	Eph. 6:11–13
2	Wear the shoes of peace	Eph. 6:15
3	The sword of the Spirit *(using God's Word)*	Eph. 6:17
4	Prayer	Eph. 6:18
5	Evangelism	2 Cor. 4:3–6
6	Casting out demons	Matt. 10:1
7	Tithing and giving	Mal. 3:8–12
8	Worship and praise	Acts 16:25–28
9	Resisting Satan's schemes	James 4:7
10	Humility	1 Pet. 5:5–7
11	Fasting	Matt. 6:16–18
12	Disciple making	Matt. 28:19–20

Wearing the full armor

The soldier dresses himself for battle for two reasons—to be prepared defensively and offensively for all levels of combat. The armor protects him from the enemy's attacks while also giving him an offensive edge in unseating the enemy. The full armor must be worn at all times. The offensive perspective is that you should always be ready to seize an opportunity to take back anything the evil one has stolen from you. Don't just idly wait around protecting your stuff from Satan. Initiate an attack against him in the name of the Lord.

> **Staying alert means we never underestimate our opponent.**

Wear the shoes of peace

Paul pointed to the Roman soldier's shoes to make a strong reference to a particular area of the Christian armor in spiritual warfare. The soldier's shoes were studded with thick nails, similar to cleats football players wear today. These shoes allowed the soldiers to dig in so they did not slip during hand-to-hand combat. Similarly our spiritual shoes have been fitted with peace so we are not tossed around during difficult times.

In Romans 5:1 we are told, "Therefore, since we have been justified through faith, we have peace with God through our Lord Jesus Christ." Our peace *with* God enables us to have a settled heart when it comes to our eternal destiny. Heaven will be our next and last stop after death. Peace with God assures us we no longer have to struggle with matters like self-forgiveness, self-condemnation, or God's wrath triggered by sin. We have been forgiven. God made peace with us when we accepted Christ as our Savior. When we're dressed for battle with the peace of God, it buttresses us against Satan's accusations.

The sword of the Spirit

The spiritual weapon depicted by the metaphor "the sword of the Spirit" (Eph. 6:17) conveys the point that we can and should use Scripture to make progress in our relationship with God and in our fight against the powers of this dark world. This occurs by making confession—in this case, saying the same thing God says in His Word. I'm not referring to making confession regarding our personal sin but to making confession about what God desires. Whether you're confessing God's Word about a nation's political unrest or destructive behaviors within your own family, these can be broken by a declaration of truth. Speak God's Word over your life and let it do its work.

Each time her daughter Debbie put on her short skirts and makeup for another night of clubbing, Becky had a regular confession she would say to her unsaved daughter: "God is going to take away the pleasure you get from clubbing. You are going to serve the Lord and even preach His Word." Today Debbie is an ordained minister in the Bronx, New York, and she testifies in her sermons how angry she became when her mom used the sword of the Spirit to discourage her from clubbing. But, she admits, it was a powerful weapon—leading her to reject her partying ways and begin seeking God.

Prayer

Prayer is both a defensive and offensive spiritual weapon. An example of an offensive prayer can be seen in Acts 13:1–3 when Paul, Barnabas, and the other elders at the church of Antioch gathered for a special time of seeking God. This time of intercession resulted in a wonderful prophetic moment for Paul and Barnabas as their apostolic calling was revealed to the other elders and ultimately to their congregation. Consider using the offensive weapon of prayer to make progress in any area of your life. I strongly encourage you to shut yourself away with God and pour out your hunger for development and progress before Him. You'll be pleased by the outcome.

**Speak God's Word over your life
and let it do its work.**

Evangelism

In spiritual warfare our adversary is launching vicious attacks against everybody—believers and unbelievers alike. Satan's aim is to blind the minds of unbelievers "so that they cannot see the light of the gospel of the glory of Christ" (2 Cor. 4:4). The offensive weapon of evangelism must be employed to thwart this intent.

Sharing the message of Christ's love to unbelievers is a great undertaking, but prayer evangelism, which was used by the early church, calls for a saturation of prayer before witnessing. Prayer evangelism underscores the effectiveness of prayer in readying the hearts of unbelievers to embrace the truth of the gospel. A heightened sensitivity to God's forgiveness found in Jesus Christ allows the time of witnessing to become more fruitful.

Prayer evangelism is an offensive weapon you should begin using today. Make a list of people for whom you're particularly burdened. Begin praying tactically for their openness to the gospel. Ask God to lead you to share His message with them at an opportune time. Satan's kingdom suffers a tremendous blow whenever more people join God's family and turn their backs on him forever.

Casting out demons

When Jesus drove a demon out of a man, He was accused of driving out demons by Beelzebub—the prince of demons (Matt. 12:24). To defend His offensive actions against the kingdom of darkness Jesus simply posed an instructional question: "How can anyone enter a strong man's house and carry off his possessions unless he first ties up the strong man?" (v. 29). Casting out demons is a powerful way to offensively attack Satan's kingdom and diminish the number of his followers.

Tithing and giving

Who would have thought that tithing and giving are offensive weapons of spiritual warfare? Only God in His infinite wisdom would have included such an unexpected benefit to such an ordinary practice. The prophet Malachi pronounced God's design when he shared that a by-product of tithing—giving one-tenth of our income to the work of the Lord—would cause God to rebuke the devourer for us (Mal. 3:8–12, NKJV). The word *rebuke* means "to speak harshly," "to strongly correct," and "to express stern disapproval." Imagine this: you simply honor God with your tithe, and He sternly tells Satan to back off of your life and stuff. What a powerful weapon! If you haven't been using this weapon, begin rearranging your financial life so your local church will benefit from your tithe while you benefit from God's protection of your goods against satanic attacks.

Prayer evangelism underscores the effectiveness of prayer in readying the hearts of unbelievers to embrace the truth of the gospel.

Worship and praise

This offensive weapon is illustrated when Paul and Silas were imprisoned for driving a demon out of a young woman. Facing public humiliation and the aftermath of being wrongly jailed, the two men began worshipping and praising the Lord (Acts 16:25–37). God responded by opening the jail doors supernaturally and by softening the heart of the jailer to the gospel message. Worship and praise become offensive weapons when you intentionally initiate singing to God because His goodness is everywhere—even in prison. As the apostles sang, the feelings of despair that Satan had tried to pour into their souls were dispelled. The weapon of praise was used offensively to free them from imprisonment.

Resisting Satan's schemes

To overcome spiritual assaults we are required to submit to God and to resist the devil. To *resist* is "to stand against," "to oppose," and "to withstand the devil's plans." Resisting Satan begins with an attitude of opposition; then it moves to prayer-filled action to withstand anything contrary to God's will. This act of resisting sends the signal to the kingdom of darkness that this is war.

José, a friend, shared with me one morning over coffee how he escaped the jaws of temptation though admittedly he was flattered at first. Sally was married and very attractive. She began flirting with José by paying him seemingly innocent compliments about his clothing and cologne. Then she made it perfectly clear she was willing to make good on her advances toward him. As a new believer and a single man José knew nothing good could come of Sally's advances. She needed to work out her marital issues without looking to him for intimacy. José felt good about himself because he successfully resisted Satan's scheme to trap him in a sexual web.

Humility

Because pride comes before a fall, humility is a trait Peter instructs us to develop. If we fail to heed this warning, we may quickly find ourselves being opposed by God and falling prey to Satan's schemes (1 Pet. 5:5–7). The great English preacher Dr. D. Martyn Lloyd-Jones is often quoted as saying, "The worst thing that can happen to a man is to succeed before he is ready."[3] Pride is the playpen of the devil. It makes us rely solely on our own strength, gifting, and wisdom. That's why Satan tosses proud people around like there's no tomorrow. Avoid this assault by pursuing humility at all costs.

> **The act of resisting sends the signal to the kingdom of darkness that this is war.**

My friend Henry strongly disapproved of his adult daughter's decisions and told her so in no uncertain terms. She had been distancing herself from her mother to please her husband's anti-family behavior. There was a lot of truth to what Henry said to her, but he did not want his pride to get in the way of her healing or to become a wedge in her relationship with her husband. As a tactical and offensive move, Henry recognized how humility would expedite his prayers for her to walk with Christ and reconnect with her mother.

Fasting

Jesus practiced fasting as a discipline and instructed us to do the same (Matt. 6:16–18). When you decide to abstain from eating for a set period of time to draw closer to God, it has a powerful and offensive impact against Satan's kingdom. Fasting is always coupled with prayer, though it stands as a distinctly different practice. According to the New Testament, there is no set regimen we must adhere to when using this offensive weapon. However, we cannot ignore Jesus's assumption when He said, "When you fast…" (v. 16). He inferred that we ought to include fasting as a spiritual discipline if we want to achieve maximum success.

I have enjoyed a life of fasting for some thirty years. The rewards have been tremendous. Whenever I feel spiritually empty or lazy in my pursuit of God, I begin a time of fasting. Most times I fast at least one day per week. My goal is constantly to make progress in the pursuit of God's purposes for this generation.

Disciple making

The Great Commission compels us not only to evangelize but also to make disciples of those who accept the message of Jesus (Matt. 28:19–20). The process of making disciples is more arduous than winning souls. Disciple-makers hold the hands of new converts to ensure they mature in their relationship with Christ. This is an offensive tool in spiritual warfare. The stronger the Christian becomes, the more he will defeat Satan wherever he tries to rear his ugly head. Ask God to help you become a disciple-maker. Then take the time to learn, grow, and help others along the way to spiritual maturity. In so doing, you help defeat Satan in a vital way.

Making a decision to become a professional soldier is of paramount importance. Take the time to review the defensive and offensive weapons as often as needed. Gaining experience in using these weapons all at once may initially appear daunting. But if you are going to be a successful kneeling warrior, you must become extremely skillful with these weapons. There's no way that goal can be reached if you continue basking in the comfort of civilian life. You must take the plunge and become a professional full-time soldier in the army of the Lord.

Chapter 5

WELCOME TO THE SCHOOL OF PRAYER!

COLLEGE IS AN INTENTIONAL STEP FOR MOST STUDENTS. And with the guidance—and checkbooks—of their parents, many young adults are steered through the appropriate channels to ensure a smooth transition to higher learning.

But some of life's best lessons are learned accidentally. Consider some of the leading graduates from Jesus's school of prayer. When you look at their stories, you will find it quite surprising that these notable kneeling warriors stumbled through the doors ignorant of prayer and its power.

Even our Old Testament hero Abraham found himself on his face before God pleading for Sodom and Gomorrah. There he was interceding for the people of that destructive twin city. But only when Abraham was made privy to God's disdain for their evil did this man of God consider praying for God's wrath to be quenched. Knowing full well that his nephew Lot lived in Sodom, Abraham began to intercede for the city by default.

The night Abraham's grandson Jacob wrestled all night for the Lord to change the murderous heart of his brother, Esau, he enrolled in the school of prayer.

Another graduate of the school of prayer was Queen Esther. When challenged by her cousin Mordecai to ask her husband, King Xerxes, to spare the lives of the Jews living in Babylon, she stumbled upon the power of prayer. This spiritual confrontation led Esther into a three-day period of fasting and prayer for the king's favor. The threat of Esther's annihilation and that of her fellow Jewish people proved to be her enrollment in the school of prayer.

> **Enrollment in the school of prayer is commonly triggered by pain that stems from an overwhelming personal need.**

It was happenstance even for the great apostle Paul. We find this broken man on his face before God for three consecutive days. Why? Paul had come face-to-face with the reality that his entire spiritual and theological worldview was out of sync with God. Profoundly impacted by a vision of Jesus as he was traveling on the road to Damascus, this convicted sinner turned to God in prayer (Acts 9:1-19). Paul was not just blind spiritually; the vision of Jesus blinded him physically. Paralyzed by the thought of "How should I live now?", Paul had no recourse but to enroll in the school of prayer. He had to get things right with God and right in his soul. To help him along, God sent a trusted disciple by the name of Ananias to pray that he would regain his sight. The Lord told Ananias, "Go to the house of Judas on Straight Street and ask for a man from Tarsus named Saul, *for he is praying*" (v. 11, emphasis added). This future powerhouse and apostle in the Lord's church entered the sacred halls of the school of prayer through the doorway marked *Damascus Road Experience.*

You probably tripped into the school of prayer just as I did. There is no need to feel awkward about it. I can't think of any great biblical, historical, or contemporary intercessor who has entered those sacred halls of prayer studies other than by accident. Enrollment is commonly triggered by pain that stems from an overwhelming personal need. Paul puts it this way: "The pain turned you to God" (2 Cor. 7:9, TLB). How right he was. C. S. Lewis, the great English philosopher, provides this insight to the gift of pain: "God whispers to us in our pleasures, speaks in our consciences, but shouts in our pains. It is his megaphone to rouse a deaf world."[1]

I'm not sure why it takes such excruciating pain for us to become interested in prayer...real prayer. Yet God patiently waits for His people to visit His throne room. And, when they get around to it, the visit for many becomes a permanent residency and not an overnight stay.

ENROLLING IN
THE SCHOOL OF PRAYER

Hannah was overwhelmed for years with her barrenness. But when the pain became unbearable, she turned to God in prayer. First Samuel chapter 1 captures a most fascinating story of her enrollment in the school of prayer and the common lesson every kneeling warrior must learn: how to prevail in prayer. This ordinary woman wanted what every Jewish wife desired. She wanted to produce a son for her husband. Although Elkanah had a second wife, Peninnah, who had many sons and daughters, Hannah was his favorite. Yet Hannah did not have a child, much less a son.

> **Prevailing prayer is mighty, fervent, and persuasive. It is designed to lift heavy, burdensome loads off your shoulders and place them at the Lord's feet.**

Each year Elkanah and his family made the journey to Shiloh to worship and sacrifice to the Lord. Most scholars agree that this was the time of the year when the Feast of Tabernacles was celebrated. Peninnah seized this moment annually to tease Hannah about her infertility—fully aware it signified the ultimate tragedy for a married woman in the Hebrew culture. The happiness of every Hebrew husband rested on a son's birth to perpetuate his name and inherit his estate. Although Elkanah never scorned Hannah for her childlessness, it became a great indignity and deficiency in her own eyes. She desperately desired a son.

Barrenness led Hannah to the only One who could heal her—Almighty God. She learned how to pray by praying. This is exactly why Dick Eastman writes in the book *No Easy Road*: "To learn prayer men must pray. We learn prayer's deepest depths in prayer, not from books. We reach prayer's highest in prayer, not from sermons."[2] Hannah's prayer for a son was not just any ordinary prayer. It embodied the type of prayer that warriors learn and become skilled at during tough times. It is *prevailing prayer.*

If you're going to graduate from the school of prayer and enjoy the status of a kneeling warrior, you must know the dynamics of prevailing prayer. Learn it. Use it. Master it. Prevailing prayer is mighty, fervent, and persuasive. It is designed to lift heavy, burdensome loads off your shoulders and place them at the Lord's feet. You will know when you've entered into this space and prevailed successfully before God because there are signs—unmistakable indicators—to alert you of your arrival.

PREVAILING PRAYER IS PERSONAL

Until you personally feel the need to cry out to God, you will not prove to be mighty, fervent, or persuasive in prayer. You must own the need. The need must be real to you. You must personally pursue an audience with God. He has all the answers to *your* dilemma. Turn to the Lord and let Him show Himself mighty on *your* behalf.

I saw firsthand the power of prevailing prayer. Eight years after my wife and I planted Christ Church, the congregation was still meeting in rental facilities. In fact, we held worship in six different rental facilities ranging from a hotel, restaurant, and a multipurpose room of a church to a catering hall during that time. Most of the moves occurred without any forewarning by the property owners. In one case we were told on a Friday morning that the owners of the catering hall we were renting had filed bankruptcy and we could not use their facility any longer. The pressure to find a meeting place by Sunday had to be met by nothing short of a miracle from God. We found one, but because the restaurant was so large with simultaneous parties during our worship time, we only met there for one month. Plus, our vibrant worship was a distraction to wedding parties and other social functions. Understandably we had to move. All those moves tested us emotionally and physically. Each week the men of the church set up and broke down all the sound equipment, arranged the chairs, and temporarily repositioned items in the room to form a comfortable short-term sanctuary. The women worked right alongside us, unloading the entire curriculum for children's church and staging our makeshift sanctuaries with banners, flowers, and so on.

New Jersey is very densely populated. In Northern New Jersey, just outside of New York City, finding a building offering seating for five hundred to a thousand people is like trying to find water in the desert. We scoured the region for years to no avail. Finally, in 1994—our eighth year of ministry—a Realtor called me and said, "Rev. Ireland, I found a building that has not yet hit the multiple listing catalog. It's an old cathedral in the township of Montclair. Can you meet me at the intersection of Church Street and Trinity Place in about thirty minutes?" I quickly said, "Yes," and drove like a maniac to what would be our future home. My need for a building had become personal. Although our church had grown to approximately five hundred people, I was still facing the periodic remarks made by some visitors and others in the community who defined a "real church" by building ownership. In their minds we were not yet "a real or healthy church" since we owned no real estate and could not be identified with a physical building.

When I pulled up in front of the cathedral, it looked like one huge monstrosity. I could tell that it had been a beautiful site in its heyday and that it had brought a sense of pride to the community. But the sight standing before me was ghastly. The trees were infested with ticks and lice. There was no grass on the property—only bare dirt. And those were the good features! When I walked through the doors, I thought I had accidentally entered the television set of the old *The Addams Family* show. The interior was ominous and broken down. Plaster was falling everywhere. The building's bell tower, which soared some one hundred feet into the sky, was leaking, and plaster and other debris were scattered on the floor beneath.

The building's main sanctuary seated approximately nine hundred people, including the balcony, but it too needed a lot of tender loving care—to say the least. There were eight light fixtures hanging from the sixty-foot high ceiling. Each fixture held about eight tiny twenty-five-watt bulbs, rendering the large sanctuary frighteningly dark and dreary.

In addition to the fact that the structure was so dilapidated, there were many different groups renting out space in the building. The owners—the First Baptist Church of Montclair—used a small chapel for their meetings. A Jewish synagogue used the larger fellowship hall. There was also a Pentecostal church, a day care center, an Eastern mystical group, and a food bank among other smaller groups using rooms in the building. It was like Mecca—with all roads leading to God.

But my personal need for a building kept me pressing forward. Before I even got halfway through the tour, I heard myself say, "I'll take it!" Then I remembered to ask: "How much is it?" He answered, "It is $1.25 million. It's a steal!" In agreement with his opinion, I said, "OK, I'll offer them full price." I signed the contract that Friday morning. Afterward the Realtor said, "Rev, please bring the first part of the down payment, which is one hundred thousand dollars, on Monday." "Sure!" I said, without a clue as to how I'd make good on my promise.

As I walked to my car, the thought hit me like a ton of bricks: "We don't have one hundred thousand dollars. We don't even have ten thousand dollars. What have I done? What are we going to do?" The only thing I knew to do was to enter into prevailing prayer. You'd better believe my prayer was *passionate*. And it was very *precise*. I needed one hundred thousand dollars by Monday—only three days away. My prayer was also *personal*. I needed a building for my growing congregation.

After the first hour of prevailing in prayer, the only impression I received from the Holy Spirit was to circulate a special announcement to our members. I asked my small staff to contact our small group leaders, who would be instructed to telephone each member of their small group. The phone calls would only reveal that Pastor David had a special announcement to share on Sunday and that everyone was encouraged to come to worship. No one other than our pastoral team knew what my announcement would be.

After delivering that instruction, I returned to my prayer closet to continue crying out before God. I needed one hundred thousand dollars by Sunday, and this was Friday afternoon. The second impression I received in prayer was to hire a photographer to take a specific shot of the building. The thought was that faith would be ignited in the hearts of the people if they could get a glimpse of the grandness of this structure. My problem, however, was that the building was an eyesore. I met the photographer at the building and led him to the balcony. I asked him to angle his camera in a particular way so that he would get a shot of the only thing that looked good in the building—the beautiful stained glass window at the rear of the altar. This picturesque rose window looked fantastic—especially around two o'clock in the afternoon when the sun was at its brightest. The rich reds, blues, and amber colors were boldly illuminated in every detail of the magnificent sixty feet by thirty feet stained glass.

The photographer followed my lead by ensuring that the shot didn't capture the ugly, dimly lit, cobweb-covered chandeliers. I asked him to develop seven hundred copies of a five-by-seven photo. Armed with the photos I returned to the prayer closet to continue prevailing in prayer.

I prayed for several more hours over the course of Friday and Saturday, pouring out my soul to the Lord. When Sunday morning rolled around, I still didn't have a clue as to what I was going to do. All I knew was that I needed one hundred thousand dollars cash on Monday or we'd forfeit the building—the only one I was able to find after eight years of searching. Although I drove off to church that morning uncertain as to *how* I was going to get the one hundred thousand dollars for the Lord's work, I had a peace birthed through prayer that the money would absolutely be there that morning.

The Essex Manor catering hall was buzzing with excitement that Sunday morning. After the worship portion of our service, I walked onto the platform and greeted the people. I could feel their thoughts: "OK enough with the greeting. What do you want to share with us, Pastor?" I responded by announcing in a celebrative tone: "I've found a building! Ushers, pass out the photos!" When everyone saw the photo of the majestic stained glass window, the place erupted in praise. Some were dancing in the aisles, others were jumping up and down in front of their seats, and others were crying and thanking God aloud; even the conservative people were displaying their exuberance.

After about ten minutes of celebrative cheers, shouts, and singing, I calmed everyone down with these words: "There's just one little item that we must settle today." I pointed to the back doors—the doors that lead to exiting the room—and said, "Before I walk out of those double doors today, I need one hundred thousand dollars cash." The room became eerily quiet. The silence was suddenly broken by the unmistakable sound of people ripping the photos in futility as if to say, "There goes that!" Out of nowhere came these words out of my mouth: "Don't worry! All we need is in the house!" It was as if God was speaking through me. I had an assurance from the Holy Spirit that the money we needed to solidify this purchase was in the room.

Fervent and mighty prayer is birthed in the pain and anguish of your lack—which can only be alleviated by prayer.

Emboldened by this reality, I quickly asked that two people who could give five thousand dollars to stand to their feet. Amazingly two people stood up. The next moment I heard myself say, "I need five people who can give twenty-five hundred dollars; please stand." Instantly five people stood up. Again I was shocked. I followed this same format, decreasing the increments, and in less than ten minutes we had one hundred thousand dollars cash. The congregation went into an uproar giving thanks to God.

Fervent and mighty prayer is birthed in the pain and anguish of your lack—which can only be alleviated by prayer. Hannah lived in a constant state of spiritual defeat. She was personally fed up with her barrenness and being the source of Peninnah's provocation. The pain of barrenness was part of *her* personal feelings. And the feelings of misery, depression, and emotional emptiness were included in *her* personal feelings.

Having a wealthy husband, evidenced by Elkanah having two wives, wasn't enough for Hannah. Money did not replace the need of engaging *her* motherly instincts with a child. Marital love, which Elkanah freely gave to her, was not enough to medicate *her* pain. Neither did religion with all of its rituals

115

and practices quiet Hannah's embittered soul. She deeply wanted a son. Her soul had to be poured out in prayer before God. Prevailing prayer cannot be delegated to someone else. As loving as he was, Elkanah was satisfied with the children Peninnah had borne him. Hannah had to personally enroll in the school of prayer.

The thought entered her mind that God was powerful enough to grant *her* the desires of *her* heart. Having a son would change her destiny forever. Though her desire was personal, it was not selfish. In Hannah's time of prayer the thought of having a son for her own soul's satisfaction became too limiting and too selfish. She qualified her prayer with the promise to God: "If you will only look upon your servant's misery and remember me, and not forget your servant but give her a son, then I will give him to the LORD for all the days of his life" (1 Sam. 1:11).

Hannah openly confessed *her* misery. She freely acknowledged *her* desire for a son. Though her prayer was personal, it was unselfish. This boy would be given to the Lord, for the Lord's work.

PREVAILING PRAYER IS PASSIONATE

Hannah lived in a barren state for a number of years. Although she was troubled, vexed, and depressed over her condition, she did not consider making it a matter of prayer. In fact, she had not even considered prayer. This is what happens to many people. Their emotions overshadow their spiritual clarity, and they don't consider God as *the* sole source of blessings, answers, and wisdom to combat their dilemma. I'd like to help you fully understand Hannah's emotional state by inviting you to become familiar with the following verses in her story.

> Year after year this man went up from his town to worship and sacrifice to the LORD Almighty at Shiloh, where Hophni and Phinehas, the two sons of Eli, were priests of the LORD. Whenever the day came for Elkanah to sacrifice, he would give portions of the meat to his wife Peninnah and to all her sons and daughters. But to Hannah he gave a double portion because he loved her, and the LORD had closed her womb. And because the LORD had closed her womb, her rival kept provoking her in order to irritate her. This went on year after year. Whenever Hannah went up to the house of the LORD, her rival provoked her till she wept and would not eat. Elkanah her husband would say to her, "Hannah, why are you weeping? Why don't you eat? Why are you downhearted? Don't I mean more to you than ten sons?"
>
> —1 SAMUEL 1:3–8

It's clear that Hannah had fallen prey to an unhealthy emotional state. People in the throes of natural challenge often overlook prayer as a solution. Many are simply too emotionally distraught to think about prayer. Their pain gets the best of them. Others don't pray because they lack faith in God. Still others shy away from prayer, real prayer, because they are out of alignment with God. They don't observe the areas of obedience God requires such as confession of sin and putting Christ first in their lifestyle practices, but obedience is big on God's list of requirements for answered prayers. That's why John writes:

"If we confess our sins, he is faithful and just and will forgive us our sins and purify us from all unrighteousness" (1 John 1:9). God makes establishing alignment with Him easy. A simple yet heartfelt confession of your sins will automatically give you complete access to the Lord and all of His power.

Early and often is the best way to describe my confession of sin. I've learned over the years that it's best to ask God to forgive my sins as soon as I am aware of them. I don't want to live in broken fellowship with Jesus. I know sin creates the first hairline crack in my relationship with Him, and the gap grows wider and wider the longer it takes me to confess my sins before Him. So I'm regularly going before God, confessing, repenting, and forsaking any sins—even the ones I have committed unknowingly. In the way that we must keep current our car payments, mortgage notes, and other financial obligations to remain in good standing with our debtors, we must keep our confessions of sins current to remain in good standing with God. This gives us full confidence that our holy and loving Father will enjoy answering our prayers.

Something shifted with Hannah that day in the temple. She turned her tears into liquid prayers. Her depression morphed into passionate praying. She no longer was going to try to medicate her troubled heart with spiritually empty mourning and fasting. She decided to fight for her destiny through prayer. She entered into the school of prayer, stating that she was "pouring out my soul to the LORD" (1 Sam. 1:15). Hannah became passionate about her need!

> In bitterness of soul Hannah wept much and prayed to the LORD. And she made a vow, saying,

"O LORD Almighty, if you will only look upon your servant's misery and remember me, and not forget your servant but give her a son, then I will give him to the LORD for all the days of his life, and no razor will ever be used on his head."

As she kept on praying to the LORD, Eli observed her mouth. Hannah was praying in her heart, and her lips were moving but her voice was not heard. Eli thought she was drunk and said to her, "How long will you keep on getting drunk? Get rid of your wine."

"Not so, my lord," Hannah replied, "I am a woman who is deeply troubled. I have not been drinking wine or beer; I was pouring out my soul to the LORD. Do not take your servant for a wicked woman; I have been praying here out of my great anguish and grief."

Eli answered, "Go in peace, and may the God of Israel grant you what you have asked of him."

—1 SAMUEL 1:10–17

Something shifted with Hannah that day in the temple. She turned her tears into liquid prayers. Her depression morphed into passionate praying.

Some nine months after she passionately made her plea to the Lord, Hannah embraced a baby boy, Samuel. After he was weaned, Hannah kept her promise by giving him to the Lord. Samuel remained in Shiloh with Eli and became one of the mightiest prophets in Israel's history. Prevailing prayer is passionate praying because it is precise! Although prevailing prayer is designed to lift a heavy load from your heart, it is a singular load.

PREVAILING PRAYER IS PRECISE

Persuasive prayer requires singular focus. It is precise, with a laser-like sensor. Like most people Hannah had many needs, but the one that most consumed her mind was her barrenness. Hannah prayed for a son. Charles Finney, the famed American evangelist, writes: "The Spirit leads Christians to desire and pray for things of which nothing is specifically said in the word of God."[3] As Finney underscores, God placed the desire for a son on Hannah's heart. That desire made her prayer both focused and precise.

Determining that you're going to pray until you are assured your voice was heard on high cannot be done in the shower or while driving to work. Prevailing praying takes time.

Prevailing prayer is also seen in the Garden of Gethsemane when Jesus prayed: "My Father, if it is possible, may this cup be taken from me. Yet not as I will, but as you will" (Matt. 26:39). Jesus's prayer was specific. His singular request was for the coming crucifixion, evidenced in the metaphor of the cup, to be removed from Him. As He continued praying in the garden, He made the same particular request on two other occasions. After each request He walked over to the three disciples—Peter,

James, and John—to find them sleeping instead of praying. After encouraging them to remain in prayer, he went back to prevailing in prayer. Altogether He made three separate requests, all with the same precise plea: "My Father, if it is not possible for this cup to be taken away unless I drink it, may your will be done" (v. 42).

Prevailing prayer is strictly defined by the kneeling warrior pouring out his troubled soul before God. Our souls are troubled by one particular thing over all others when this kind of prayer is offered. Before Jesus began to pray, He said to the three men, "My soul is overwhelmed with sorrow to the point of death" (v. 38). Likewise, before Hannah began to pray, she was depressed. Her precision in prayer was borne out of this "bitterness of soul" (1 Sam. 1:10). Your emotional burden becomes the sole topic in prevailing prayer. Your passionate plea to God is fueled by the strong emotions you feel concerning the subject of prayer. Don't ignore or downplay the role that your emotions play when you pray. God captures the power of your emotions as part of your prayer. Jesus displayed His emotions of sorrow just as Hannah displayed her emotions of anguish. On both occasions their emotions were in sync with their impassioned words of prayer. And they both prevailed before God.

PREVAILING PRAYER IS PURPOSEFUL

Hannah's prayer had a larger purpose than to simply result in her coddling a son. As she was prevailing in prayer, she thought about God's kingdom. So she vowed to give her son to the Lord all the days of his life. Her desire was to see a priest who would truly represent God in the way he carried himself. Hannah committed her son to live as a Nazirite from birth when she vowed, "And no razor will ever be used on his head" (v. 11). A Nazirite was one who dedicated himself fully to the service of the Lord by a threefold commitment. First, no razor was ever to be used on his head. Second, he would not drink any wine or other fermented drink. Third, he would not eat anything considered unclean (Lev. 10:8–9; Judg. 13:6–7). Hannah's purpose in seeking a son was to produce a man who was wholly devoted to God's work.

Another purpose behind Hannah's prayer for a son was for the betterment of the nation of Israel. Her country lacked adequate, godly leadership. The current priests—Hophni and Phinehas—two sons of Eli, were morally and spiritually corrupt. It was common knowledge throughout the land that these men slept with the women who served at the entrance to the Tent of Meeting (1 Sam. 2:22–24). Imagine that: priests so morally depraved that they slept with vulnerable women and were not even convicted when the news of their depravity became public. Hannah wanted something better for the priesthood. She wanted something far better for her nation. She prevailed in prayer with that purpose in mind.

You have to pray with the perspective that God's blessings are worth fighting for.

Equally important to Hannah was the need for a son who could model the ways of the Lord to the next generation. The next generation of Israelites was entitled to better examples of godly men than Hophni and Phinehas. As she prevailed in prayer, the thought may have loomed in her mind: nothing is more important than to pray for a purpose that is bigger than you. The idea of giving her boy to the Lord was easy because her prayer was filled with a divine purpose.

PREVAILING PRAYER IS PERSEVERING

You can't be in a hurry while waiting on God. Determining that you're going to pray until you are assured your voice was heard on high cannot be done in the shower or while driving to work. Prevailing praying takes time. Jacob wrestled *all night* with the angel of the Lord. At daybreak this angel that had appeared in the form of man said to Jacob, "'Let me go, for it is daybreak.' But Jacob replied, 'I will not let you go unless you bless me'" (Gen. 32:26). Jacob's experience with prevailing prayer lasted all night. But don't be reluctant because of the time commitment needed for prevailing prayer. Its rewards will exceed any sacrifice of time you make.

The great prophet Elijah prayed seven times for rain. Each time he bent down to the ground and put his face between his knees, crying out fervently to God. Only at the end of the seventh session did he prevail (1 Kings 18:41–44). The rain came, the famine ended, and the nation experienced a deluge of blessings from God. The text provides no timetable for Elijah's seven times of prayer. But we can surmise that he was engaged in prevailing prayer. The fact that he sent his servant on seven specific occasions to look toward the sea for a cloud lets us know that the prophet persisted at his request. Like Jacob he was not going to let God go until rain came.

The identical trait of perseverance was demonstrated in

Hannah's time of prayer. After she prayed and vowed to the Lord, the Scriptures note, "She kept on praying to the Lord" (1 Sam. 1:12). Prevailing prayer is persevering prayer. Hannah needed time to pour out her soul to the Lord. This can only happen when distractions are dismissed and you connect emotionally and spiritually with the Lord. There are times I enter into prayer only to find that my mind is cluttered with the affairs of the day. Only after I free my mind from diversions do I have a meaningful and effective time in prayer.

You have to pray with the perspective that God's blessings are worth fighting for. Hannah knew deep within her heart that God rewards those who diligently seek after Him in prayer (Heb. 11:6). The thought of prevailing in prayer originates with God. We are invited by the Holy Spirit to fervently plead our case before the court of heaven. God would not create a hunger within us for something He never plans to feed. Hannah's cry for a son was first born in the heart of God. It was He who had "closed her womb" (1 Sam. 1:5), and it would be He who would open it.

Hannah persisted in prayer, and it matured her. She now knew God more intimately. Her relationship with God transformed from theoretical and speculative to one that was practical and relational.

Prevailing Prayer Is Powerful

Prevailing prayer proved powerful enough to lift the heaviness of Hannah's infertility from her life. Her countenance was no longer heavy and sullen. The load of her troubled soul was poured out before the Lord. After she prevailed before

God, "she went her way and ate something, and her face was no longer downcast" (v. 18). The power of this kind of prayer is that it moves God. Hannah was full of hope—the God kind of hope. Her reliance was not in her strength or Elkanah's virility as a man. Hannah's confidence rested in God's power.

How do you know when to cease prevailing prayer? When you receive the peace in your heart that the answer has been granted.

No longer would Hannah be emotionally derailed by Peninnah. She was filled with the peace of God secured in her time of prayer. Prevailing prayer was powerful enough to anchor her faith to the One who is unmovable. The Lord Almighty had deeply assured her that the matter was settled in the courts of heaven. Her case had been fervently and effectively pleaded. Her mighty and persuasive words, stemming from a heart of sacrifice and concern for the kingdom of God, proved powerful.

The matter was forever settled. There was no further need to pray again about this topic. As Jesus said to His three disciples in the Garden of Gethsemane, "Rise, let us go!" (Matt. 26:46). He had powerfully prevailed in prayer. As Elijah told his servant to tell Ahab after he saw the cloud rising from the sea, "Hitch up your chariot and go down before the rain stops you" (1 Kings 18:44). In other words, "I don't need to pray about rain any further; I have prevailed with God."

The question we must all answer is this: How do you know when to cease prevailing prayer? There's only one answer: you stop praying when you receive the peace in your heart that the answer has been granted. Remember, prevailing prayer began with a passionate need that went unmet in your life. Your emotions became full and overwhelming. This conveyed a deep need only God could meet. Similarly your emotions will feel satisfied when you have moved God in prayer. You will feel that the emotional need has been met, even if the actual promise tarries for a while. In Hannah's case, the baby boy arrived "in the course of time" (1 Sam. 1:20), or as the Jewish historian Flavius Josephus noted, "when they had returned to their own country"[4] she discovered she was pregnant.

An inner sense of peace makes it perfectly clear you no longer need to pray about the issue. It has been settled by God. Live in the peace that you have moved God and that the heavy load has been lifted. You have graduated from the school of prayer as a kneeling warrior. The requirement for graduation has been met. You've succeeded in the art of prevailing prayer.

Chapter 6

THE ART OF
SPIRITUAL WARFARE

WHEN YOU WITNESS THE SKILL OF ELITE FIGHTERS, it looks as if you're watching a well-choreographed performance. They have spent countless hours practicing specific drills to become adept at the use of specific fighting techniques. When the actual contest occurs, their movement is graceful and appears effortless. These expert fighters know the moves and countermoves they must make to defeat their opponent. In the same way we must strive to become skilled at the art of spiritual warfare. To reach that pinnacle, we must know the ins and outs of the fighting techniques Jesus taught.

Frances was a single parent and a faithful member of my congregation. It had become increasingly difficult for her to maintain a healthy relationship with her teenage daughter, Becky. Becky had become combative, sassy, and distant. Every conversation Frances had with Becky resulted in a fight. If Frances asked Becky to go with her to church, she would go berserk. But just a few years prior Becky had been a warm, compassionate child who loved going to church. Now she'd begun listening to a form of rock music that sounded almost demonic and horrifying. Becky started piercing her ears then parts of her face. She became depressed and withdrawn and began hating herself. Her mother reported, "I lost all access to her." Even after graduating from high school and getting an academic scholarship to college, Becky still hated herself and remained in a deep depression.

This dark sadness even affected her menstrual cycle. In fact, it had stopped altogether. Her lips even changed colors. Their family doctor couldn't detect what was wrong even after several blood tests were conducted. Finally Frances became furious about what Satan was doing. He was trying to kill her daughter, trying to take away their relationship, and trying to steal Becky's future. Frances told Becky, "You and I must agree in prayer for God to work a miracle for you." To Frances's surprise Becky joined her. They read Paul's description of spiritual warfare found in the sixth chapter of Ephesians. Becky realized she was undergoing a spiritual assault by Satan. Mother and daughter began to cry out to God for His help. In two days

Becky's lips regained their natural color, and her menstrual cycle began again.

God's miracle didn't stop there. Since Becky realized God cared about her, she said yes to her mother's invitation to attend Prayerfest—an annual meeting our church hosts involving dedicating an entire day to calling on God in prayer. The meeting includes worship, instructional classes on prayer, prayer walks on our campus, and powerful periods of corporate intercession that bring us to our knees, weeping before a loving God. We pray for our nation, families, and communities. We break for a couple of hours and come back at night for a special service we call "An Encounter With God." Frances invited her daughter to the evening service. That night Becky rededicated her life to Christ, and the power of depression was broken as I prayed for her.

The whole congregation wept as Frances shared what God had done for this precious young lady. Two weeks later I received a letter from Frances saying: "I got my daughter back. Our relationship has been restored. Thank God for answering our prayers." I was honored to be a witness to the power of God in winning back the life of a dear believer through spiritual warfare.

Jesus presented three powerful spiritual warfare techniques to His disciples. They centered on how we ought to pray when something is missing from our lives or when something is hindering our access to the promises of God. The parable of the friend at midnight tells of a man who received an unexpected visitor late one night. Middle Eastern culture dictated that a meal must be served to guests, and bread had to be part of the meal because bread in those days was used like cutlery in our day. It was used as an eating utensil to sop up meat and gravy. Since the man didn't have any bread, he went to a neighbor— a friend—and requested three loaves. It was midnight, and the friend and his family were in bed. Even after some persistent knocking, the friend called out that he would not get up to give the man any bread, but the man was quite shameless and boldly persisted with his knocking. So his friend reluctantly got up and gave him the three loaves of bread.

The parable concludes with this point of instruction: "So I say to you: Ask and it will be given to you; seek and you will find; knock and the door will be opened to you. For everyone who asks receives; he who seeks finds; and to him who knocks, the door will be opened" (Luke 11:9–10). Ask, seek, and knock are three critical prayer techniques. Each provides a key to securing an answer when used by a kneeling warrior. The man who had the loaves repeatedly denied his friend the bread. Yet the friend continued asking, continued seeking, and continued knocking until the door opened and he was handed three loaves of bread.

Jesus said we are to ask, and the request will be received. The word *seek* means to search, to pursue. Since this parable comes in response to the unnamed disciple's request for Jesus to "teach us to pray" (v. 1), the three phrases—ask, seek, and knock—have to do with prayer. In the realm of prayer the word *seek* means more than to search and pursue. Here it means "to search for God and His answer using your whole heart." Your focus cannot be divided. There cannot be any distraction or diversion of your heart in your pursuit of God and His answer.

Your heart must be clean, singular, and wholly committed to the Lord. That means repentance and humility must precede your requests, petitions, and prayers. Purity of motive and a laser-like focus emerge from a heart that has been cleansed through the forsaking of one's sins.

This definition of *seek* is illustrated in a number of Bible passages where its meanings can be easily grasped. For example, during one of the visions God gave to Solomon, the Lord shared this fact about Himself: "If my people, who are called by my name, will humble themselves and pray and *seek my face* and turn from their wicked ways, then will I hear from heaven and will forgive their sins and will heal their land" (2 Chron. 7:14, emphasis added). God responds to seeking people, as long as the seeking is pure and singular in focus. The true method of seeking the Lord requires humility, repentance, and forsaking one's sins. When these elements are included in drawing near to God, Jesus promises that he who seeks will find.

Ask, seek, and knock are three critical prayer techniques. Each provides a key to securing an answer when used by a kneeling warrior.

The focus of prayer in seeking the Lord was also made evident when Jeremiah prophesied God's desire to the exiles of Israel as he said, "Then you will call upon me and come and pray to me, and I will listen to you. *You will seek me* and find me when you *seek me with all your heart*" (Jer. 29:12–13, emphasis added). More specifically, this prophecy informed the Israelites *how* to seek after God through prayer. To find God in prayer, the seeking requirement to be met is that it is done with *all* your heart. The importance of the word *seek* is reinforced by Solomon and Jeremiah in that to *seek* is *to search for God and His answer with your whole heart*. This is the second of the three spiritual warfare techniques we must master.

Jesus also told His disciples that anyone who asks receives; he who seeks finds; and to him who *knocks*, the door will be opened. The word *knock* means more than just a simple rapping on a door. Since the word is being used in the context of prayer, its meaning must have a prayer focus just as the other two warfare techniques have. The phrase *knock* implies *the engaging of your faith through warfare praying, fasting, praying with a partner, and the like* until the door is opened to you. Although the phrase *knock* is not seen elsewhere in the Bible in reference to prayer, the principle and technique is noted elsewhere. For example, during an economically devastating time in the nation of Israel the prophet Joel prophesied instructionally to the elders:

> Put on sackcloth, O priests, and mourn;
>> wail, you who minister before the altar.
> Come, spend the night in sackcloth,
>> you who minister before my God;
> for the grain offerings and drink offerings
>> are withheld from the house of your God.
> Declare a holy fast;
>> call a sacred assembly.
> Summon the elders
>> and all who live in the land

to the house of the LORD your God,
and cry out to the LORD.

—JOEL 1:13–14

Spiritual warfare occurs when we experience resistance to the will of God.

The principle and meaning of *knock* is seen in these verses. The prophet urged the elders and spiritual leaders to use their faith by fasting, crying out to God, praying corporately, and even praying all night for God's provision to be released. The need was great, and the only way they would be assured of the blessing was by entering the highest level of spiritual warfare— knocking until the door of provision opens.

Jesus taught us to grow in the art of spiritual warfare by learning how to use these three methods to secure the blessing— ask, seek, and knock. Spiritual warfare occurs when we experience resistance to the will of God. There is only one spiritual being who is constantly instigating and churning up opposition of God's will, and that is Satan. This resistance points to the ongoing battle of good versus evil and of faith versus doubt. The battle is seen in righteousness versus sin. Spiritual warfare is apparent even through the collision of worldviews. The biblical worldview is often met with antagonism by those upholding contrary views regarding personal and civic life. Whether it is postmodernism, secular humanism, Islam, or plain old atheism, colliding worldviews also reflect a dimension of spiritual warfare.

Despite the genesis of spiritual warfare, we are taught to

not back down but to engage the enemy through prayer. These three prayer techniques are powerful when properly used. In chapter 20 of the Book of Judges we see an excellent example of all three techniques being used to receive answer to prayer and to secure God's blessings.

> **Spiritual warfare calls for spiritual**
> ***and* natural action.**

ASK AND YOU WILL RECEIVE

This story is set during the period in Israel's history when there was no king to rule the nation. Periodically God used judges to lead the nation for an unspecified period of time. Judges such as Samuel, Gideon, Samson, and Deborah led the nation at different times. During a phase when there was no judge, a Levite was taking his wife home after visiting her parents in another part of the country. The journey was long, so they stopped to spend the night in Gibeah, a city belonging to the tribe of Benjamin. A number of wicked men raped the Levite's wife all night until she died. The Levite was so horrified by this heinous crime committed by the Benjamites—men of the holy nation of Israel—that he cut her body into twelve pieces. He sent one piece to each of the twelve tribes so that justice would be dispensed in response to his wife's brutal murder (Judg. 20:4–7). For him his wife's victimization was a national tragedy that exposed the sinful state of God's "holy" people.

Shocked, all the people gathered in unison and anger

demanding that swift justice be meted out against the Benjamites. They asked the Benjamites to give them the men who committed this murder so they could be put to death. The Benjamites refused. Instead they assembled some 26,700 men at Gibeah to fight against Israel's 400,000 troops. Imagine how seared the Benjamites' minds must have been from sinful living and alienation against God to come up with such an ill-fated plan. They were willing to violently defend rapists and murderers rather than have them experience capital punishment (vv. 12–17).

Take a step back from the Benjamites' shocking defense of the vile men. You can see that spiritual warfare must have blinded them of basic morality. Remember, spiritual warfare is always at work when you see evil fighting against good or sin opposing righteousness. The solution was not simply to wipe out the Benjamites in an all-out street brawl, though that was quite tempting. Spiritual warfare calls for spiritual and natural action. Whenever something opposes the will of God, spiritual warfare must be the first reaction. There was no doubt that the will of God was to exact justice, strong justice, against the rapists and murderers. If the Benjamites were willing to protect these men, their behavior represented an action of injustice, which is contrary to the will of God. The Benjamites had to be held accountable.

Before taking action against the Benjamites, the Israelites went up to Bethel—the house of God—to inquire of the Lord. Here is how they asked for God's guidance: "'Who of us shall go first to fight against the Benjamites?' The Lord replied, 'Judah shall go first'" (v. 18). We learn that God was in favor of Israel taking swift, strong, and lethal justice against the Benjamites. However, instead of 400,000 soldiers fighting against the 26,700 Benjamites, only the tribe of Judah should fight them. This guidance from God followed when the Israelites *asked* for His help in prayer. The first technique in spiritual warfare is to *ask*. They made their request, petition, and inquiry in prayer. God responded. Jesus taught us to ask and we will receive. They asked and received the approval of God to fight against the Benjamites with the stipulation that Judah should go first.

God is not going to provide answers, provision, or blessings for that which is outside of His will. He wants us to live within the center of His will.

To their surprise Judah lost twenty-two thousand men that day. How could they have been defeated? They had more troops! And, more importantly, didn't they receive God's approval after asking for guidance in prayer? They most certainly did. But this is the picture of spiritual warfare: we may lose a battle even in our obedience to God's directives. Yet we must know how to proceed afterward. Why did Jesus teach us that there are three warfare techniques? We can conclude that when one technique does not generate the blessing, you must move to the other technique.

Spiritual warfare involves the resistance you encounter in attempting to execute God's will or to secure God's promises. If you are out of the will of God and you're seeking God's blessings, they won't come to you. John taught that our confidence in expecting answers to our prayers is only found when we are seeking things in accordance with the will of God (1 John 5:14–15). In other words, God is not going to provide answers, provision, or blessings for that which is outside of His will. He wants us to live within the center of His will. The more we grow in intimacy with God, the more His revealed will is easily understood and wholeheartedly pursued.

When the revealed will of God is thwarted, we must stay in spiritual warfare mode. If we've asked and have not received the desired blessing, we must continue fighting until the blessing is secured. The Israelites understood this principle. It was clear to them that the will of God meant the Benjamites had to be punished for the crime committed by the men of Gibeah. Although God gave the Israelites an affirmative answer to fight the Benjamites, they lost the battle. They asked and received God's answer, but they did not secure the victory. In this instance the first technique of spiritual warfare did not secure the blessings. Don't worry or be fatally discouraged when this happens to you. Simply move on to the second combat technique.

SEEK AND YOU WILL FIND

Sometimes you find yourself on your knees because of the ineffectiveness of others, especially when seeking a solution to a dilemma. My oldest daughter, Danielle, had a demanding professor in graduate school who failed to communicate clearly. A term paper worth 30 percent of her grade was due a month into the semester. The young and inexperienced professor had given no description or explanation of her requirement for the paper other than "a term paper is due on this date." Danielle spent a few minutes in prayer seeking God for an idea. The Lord dropped an idea into her mind and she received an A for the paper. Even in little things like this prayer can be a powerful tool for gaining wisdom from the all-knowing God.

The Israelites shook off their discouragement on the battlefield that day. They kept the matter a spiritual one *first* before making it a criminal or military one. The entire Israelite company of soldiers returned to the place of prayer. Here is what happened next:

> But the men of Israel encouraged one another and again took up their positions where they had stationed themselves the first day. The Israelites went up and wept before the LORD until evening, and they inquired of the LORD. They said, "Shall we go up again to battle against the Benjamites, our brothers?" The LORD answered, "Go up against them."
>
> —JUDGES 20:22–23

Encouragement is a vital step in spiritual warfare or spiritual development. There are times you have to encourage yourself in God. That is extremely important given the value encouragement provides. Although self-encouragement is irreplaceable, during times of intense warfare it's important to connect with other kneeling warriors to gain support from many sources. Author and leadership coach John Maxwell said, "Remember, man does not live by bread alone: sometimes he needs a little buttering up."[1] This is what the Israelites did first before initiating the *seeking* phase of spiritual warfare. They encouraged one another. American philosopher George Matthew Adams said, "There are high spots in all of our lives, and most of them have come about through encouragement from someone else. I don't care how great, how famous or successful a man or woman may be, each hungers for applause."[2]

The seeking phase caused the Israelites to return to the place of prayer. This time they needed to search their hearts through repentance and humility to understand how to approach this matter of justice against the Benjamites. A pivotal question must be answered through prayer: Did they miss God? During the asking phase, did they really hear from God to fight against the Benjamites? This fundamental question had to be answered before they could move forward in another attack. At the crux of the question was their relationship with God. It's common knowledge that sin hinders us from gaining God's blessings. To move that issue off the table, the Israelites wept before the Lord until evening. Remember, the word *seek* encompasses repentance and humility as precursors to making requests and petitions in prayer to God.

Do not let pride get in the way of your pursuit of God.

The Israelites wept before the Lord. This action is common to repentance—the acknowledgment and forsaking of one's sins. The people wanted God's mind and will on this matter. They could not afford to have anything hinder their pursuit of God. Haughtiness or sin would not interfere with their spiritual quest concerning God's will.

To the Hebrew people, to weep means "to bemoan; make lamentation; mourn with tears." Whereas tears are associated with the eyes, weeping is associated with the voice. They wept aloud before the Lord. They did not let pride get in the way of their pursuit of God. Not now. They needed to know the mind and will of God. The resistance they encountered with the loss of twenty-two thousand men showed they were up against spiritual forces of darkness and not just skillful Benjamites fighters. To break through this dark barrier and find the will and blessings of God, they had to ratchet up their spiritual weaponry to the mode of seeking God.

After self-inspection, repentance, and humility before the Lord, God spoke once again. It was clear, as was the first time: "Go up against the Benjamites." This time the Benjamites cut down eighteen thousand Israelites (Judg. 20:25). Can you believe that? How could they have lost again? It is important that we focus on the main issue whenever we engage in spiritual warfare. The main issue is the will of God. God clearly affirmed the fact that the Benjamites had to be punished for their crime against the Levite's wife. Rape and murder cannot go unpunished. The fact that the Benjamites were harboring criminals suggests that their minds, hearts, and worldview were totally opposed to that of the kingdom of God. This opposition is proof positive that more than a crime had been committed. Spiritual warfare was also at work in this situation—blinding the minds of the Benjamites to moral clarity.

The threefold principle Jesus taught was that we ought to ask, seek, and knock. The final phase of knocking held the answer to the Israelites' dilemma.

KNOCK AND THE
DOOR WILL BE OPENED

Our church planned a medical missions trip to Guatemala for over a year. Our hope was to take about fifty physicians along to provide treatment to the underserved in one of the country's poorest communities. We were able to work with a few hospitals and pharmaceutical companies in our region to secure free medicine and medical equipment. We shipped everything to Guatemala in a huge freight container. The supplies arrived safely, and the team was scheduled to fly down from New Jersey in a couple of weeks.

The victory must be secured in the prayer closet before it is experienced on the battlefield.

Days before the work was to begin, we learned that Guatemalan customs officials were not going to release our medical container. We attempted to help them understand the need for the goods the container held and the short timeline of our trip. They wouldn't budge. We had no other recourse but to turn to God. Our team in New Jersey cried out to God for a divine connection. After an hour or so one of the members of the team recalled meeting a Guatemalan businessman awhile back. He lived in Guatemala but visited the States for business at least once a month. We made contact with him, and he was sympathetic to our predicament. He noted, "Even though I'm not a Christian, you guys are doing good things for my country.

I know the wife of one of the senior government officials, and she's a Christian like you guys. I will give her a call."

On Sunday night—the day before our work was to begin—the call was made to customs. Suffice it to say that the moment the customs' official got off the phone, our container was released. Prayer works! You may not know what to do in the face of a difficult circumstance. You may not even know whom to speak to, but God is able to do amazing things when you bring these issues to Him in prayer. He knows everybody, everywhere, and has no problem making the introduction for you. Had we not knocked in prayer, some eighteen hundred people wouldn't have had their medical needs addressed during the ten-day trip.

> **We weep in response to loss and mourning. The Israelites grieved their spiritual alienation from God.**

The Israelites again encouraged themselves in the pursuit of justice and the will of God. Again, they kept the matter a spiritual one *first* before making it a criminal or military one. Here's what they did:

> Then the Israelites, all the people, went up to Bethel, and there they sat weeping before the LORD. They fasted that day until evening and presented burnt offerings and fellowship offerings to the LORD. And the Israelites inquired of the LORD. (In those days the ark of the covenant of God was there, with Phinehas son of Eleazar, the son of Aaron,

ministering before it.) They asked, "Shall we go up
again to battle with Benjamin our brother, or not?"
The LORD responded, "Go, for tomorrow I will give
them into your hands."

—JUDGES 20:26–28

The fact that they went back to Bethel to pursue God in
prayer tells us that they viewed the crisis *first* as a matter
involving spiritual warfare. The victory must be secured in the
prayer closet before it is experienced on the battlefield. Many
times we rush into battle by calling our attorney, banker, or
some other power broker rather than taking the matter *first* to
God in prayer. Kneeling warriors pray first for God's mind and
strategy before they pursue earthly solutions to their ordeal.
If this hasn't been your practice, it's essential that you put it
in place going forward. Applying this battle strategy will also
reduce your aggravation and delay. If professional services
are required, God will lead you to contact the right attorney,
accountant, or whomever. The key is understanding that you
ought to *first* take the matter to the Lord in prayer.

The principle of knocking includes the highest form of
intense praying. The Israelites sat weeping. They fasted from
morning until evening and then presented burnt offerings and
fellowship offerings to the Lord. Each action depicted the thor-
oughness they undertook in searching their hearts for any sin or
spiritual roadblocks that were deal breakers to their obtaining
the blessings of God. Each action reflected faith and tenacity in
their pursuit of God's heart.

We weep in response to loss and mourning. The Israelites
grieved their spiritual alienation from God and that of their

brother Benjamin. The fact that a Levite—a religious ruler—could have his wife raped and murdered so viciously by his own countrymen was unconscionable. The crime represented more than the wicked hearts of the men of Gibeah; it also represented the nation's apostasy. They were living separate from God's laws—those codified by Moses to guide the nation in the way of moral integrity. The shame of their desertion from God's rule and governance led to this heinous sin.

Their weeping and fasting reflected the disgust they felt toward the spiritual state of the nation and its need to return wholly to God. Fasting is a spiritual tool God designed to cleanse our inner eye—the eye of our souls that helps us see God clearly. Paul went on a three-day fast immediately after his vision of Christ blinded him on the Damascus Road (Acts 9:9). His choice to suspend eating and drinking for three days was intended to set him and his worldview on track. He had lived his entire life under the wrong set of rules and ideology. So he fasted for God's purity. The fasting was intended to purify his discernment, spiritual perspective, and to help him hear accurately from God. It worked. God heard his prayers and healed him of blindness; more importantly, God straightened out his worldview and theology. Jesus was now Lord of his life.

Likewise these Israelites needed to be completely aligned with God's view in the way they saw the Benjamites and life in general. They searched their hearts as they fasted. Anything that surfaced contrary to righteousness and holiness was repented for. They even offered burnt sacrifices and fellowship offerings, symbolic of their submission to God and their praise of Him. We learn that knocking demands intense searching of the heart to ensure that our sin and spiritual blindness are removed so that God's will is not hindered in any way. This introspection cannot be mechanical; it must be sincere and contrite. A sin-filled heart creates roadblocks to the provision of God. A clean heart is a smooth pathway to God's blessings.

> **Fasting is a spiritual tool God designed to cleanse our inner eye—the eye of our souls that helps us see God clearly.**

Unless you are desperate to reclaim your life—all facets of it—it will not happen. Maria and Georgios had migrated from Greece some twenty years ago. They fell in love back home and had a civil wedding in Athens. Some twenty-four years and three children later, their marriage was on the rocks for a number of reasons. They both had committed affairs, and Georgios had fathered a love child. They had gone to three or four Christian counselors to no avail. Their marriage was headed for divorce court. They began attending one of our church plants and scheduled a counseling session with that pastor as a last-ditch effort. They loved each other deeply despite all of the problems in their relationship.

The pastor has a passion for helping troubled couples get a full perspective of their lives together. He wisely completed a genogram with them. This instrument allows you to provide answers to questions regarding the moral choices, patterns of sin, and outcomes of your ancestors. Maria and Georgios were shocked to discover how many family members had committed affairs, fathered children out of wedlock, became victims of domestic violence, and suffered from alcohol abuse. These were also their sins. The pattern was remarkable. They recognized that they had fallen prey to the same sins of their ancestors. In fact, they shortly discovered that their oldest daughter was having an affair with a married man. The news further reinforced how a sin pattern was now taking root in their children.

Pastor Fred put together a prayer and fasting strategy for them. In a few short months their marriage began to heal. Trust began to spring back. Their daughter broke off the relationship with the man. In fact, the prayer strategy became a truth encounter—awakening the family to the reality of its situation so each member could embrace change. To celebrate their new lease on life and the reclaiming of their family, Maria and Georgios renewed their marriage vows with a huge celebration. They then took a wonderful honeymoon, which they hadn't done when they were first married. When we become desperate for our lives to be restored, prayer and fasting become invaluable tools.

There are many types of fasts. Paul used an absolute fast, which typically lasts no more than three days and involves the total abstinence of water, juice, or food. The Israelites, on the other hand, used a partial fast. They chose to not eat from morning until the evening. If you study the word *fasting* every place it's found in the Bible, you will find an abundance of practical guidance about which fast to choose based on your desired goal. More important than the type of fast you choose is the quality of the fast you undertake. When fasting, be sure to identify the desired goal and to use your regular mealtimes as times of prayer. Your prayer times will be distinctly fueled since your hunger for food is replaced with a hunger for God.

Jesus promised that when we knock, the door will be opened. This promise proved accurate with the Israelites that day. After they knocked by using their faith, weeping introspectively, practicing repentance, and the offering of sacrifices to God, they prayed, "Shall we go up again to battle with Benjamin our brother, or not?" By this time their hearts were so supple, all they wanted to do was to please God. Even if God said, "Leave the rapists and murders of Gibeah alone," the leaders would have gone home in peace, knowing they obeyed God. When you get to the technique of knocking, your heart should be so pliable in the hands of God that you have absolutely nothing to prove. Winning to you now means pleasing God. If that is not the case, you will have to go back to the beginning and relearn the warfare techniques of ask, seek, and knock in order to achieve this level of peace with the Lord.

Fortunately in this matter God wanted justice against the Benjamites. Winning the spiritual battle meant punishing the men of Gibeah and those of the tribe of Benjamin who dared to harbor and defend these murderers.

After the Israelites knocked, the Lord opened the door to them. The exact words were, "Go, for tomorrow I will give them into your hands" (Judg. 20:28). Victory was certain. The following day the Israelites struck down 25,100 Benjamites. Justice was served. The spiritual and natural battles were successfully won. The Lord's name was vindicated. The Levite received justice for his murdered wife, and the nation returned to God by restoring their moral compass.

Spiritual warfare is an art. You must know how to approach God and stay in His presence until you receive the needed strategy to secure His blessings. As Jesus taught, you can become skilled in the threefold technique of spiritual combat: ask and it will given to you; seek and you will find; knock and the door will be opened to you. If you ask and don't receive, don't worry. Move to the next level of spiritual combat, because the enemy's opposition calls for a greater effort on your part. If you seek and don't find, don't get flustered. Turn up the spiritual heat against our sly adversary by taking your warfare to the highest level of intensity. Knock, and this weapon cannot fail. The door will be opened to you.

Determine where you may have gone wrong in your last skirmish with the enemy. Perhaps you gave up after experiencing resistance though you asked God for His blessings. Armed with the truth of the Scripture, take your spiritual warfare to a new dimension by fighting for the promises of God. They are worth every second of every fight you must undergo. You are a warrior. Fight for the purpose of God for your life and this generation!

PART THREE

ENGAGE IN THE FIGHT

Chapter 7

THE WARRIORS' HUDDLE

THE NAVY SEALS NEVER LEAVE ANOTHER SEAL BEHIND on a mission. Even if a SEAL dies while in enemy territory, his brother SEALS will bring his body home. Teamwork is more than just a leadership principle to the SEALS. It's a rule that's not compromised. To underscore the importance of teamwork, SEALS are trained throughout the qualifying drills that many of their operations cannot be performed individually. A SEAL team is required to execute their functions under the assumption that all members have had the same rigorous training and skill development.

The military's work is extremely important, but its scope

is limited to earthly issues. The work of kneeling warriors has an eternal impact. The eternal consequence of the work of the kneeling warrior exceeds that of a SEAL, yet we must glean from the SEALS this all-important principle of teamwork. The SEALS didn't introduce the concept. Teamwork is stressed throughout the Bible, though we sometimes forget its importance. Thousands of years ago Solomon wrote:

> Two are better than one,
>> because they have a good return for their work:
> If one falls down,
>> his friend can help him up.
> But pity the man who falls
>> and has no one to help him up!
> Also, if two lie down together, they will keep warm.
>> But how can one keep warm alone?
> Though one may be overpowered,
>> two can defend themselves.
> A cord of three strands is not quickly broken.
>> —ECCLESIASTES 4:9–12

The benefit of corporate praying or praying in a huddle is that the request is vetted appropriately, so the will of God is certain.

The unquestioned benefit of teamwork has been presented in Scripture. There is no debate that two are better than one, especially when facing difficulty or hard work. The challenge comes in the execution of teamwork.

For Navy SEALS teamwork is developed as the members

master the same rigorous conditioning drills. I believe this is a key point for understanding the power of praying in groups. This type of prayer is often known as *the prayer of agreement.* This phrase is taken from Jesus's teaching when He said, "Again, I tell you that if two of you on earth agree about anything you ask for, it will be done for you by my Father in heaven. For where two or three come together in my name, there am I with them" (Matt. 18:19–20). The benefit of corporate praying or praying in a huddle is that the request is vetted appropriately, so the will of God is certain. Only the revealed will of God can create a passionate plea from a group of warriors.

Those in the warriors' huddle should also share the need for the request. In other words, both the need and the reward of answered prayer are shared by the group. The group legitimizes that the need is genuine and real. The group can also put their faith and power behind the request since the reward of the prayer will be paramount to them all. Jesus concluded His teaching by saying the answer from God is sure if two of you on earth agree in prayer. Kneeling warriors are able to harness remarkable power when they form a prayer huddle.

One of my earlier memories of the power of the prayer of agreement is when Christ Church had just under fifty members, with only a handful of men. I have nothing against women, but I did not want to pastor a congregation made up of well over 75 percent women. The ratio of men to women didn't reflect that of the broader society, and we all agreed it should not have been that way in God's house. All my efforts to advertise and position the church to reach men were in vain. Finally I decided to make the matter a subject of prayer. Instead of tackling it alone,

I asked the congregation to join me on a Saturday morning for the sole purpose of praying about the need for more men to join our fledgling group. To my surprise most, if not all, of the members showed up to our impromptu huddle ready to use the prayer of agreement.

We began at 9:00 a.m. and based our request on a portion of Scripture that fit our need. The prayer of agreement is almost like chipping away at a huge boulder. You have to keep addressing the matter over and over from different sides and angles until the boulder begins to crack. We prayed about the conviction of the Holy Spirit falling on our brothers, uncles, sons, fathers, and every man in our sphere of influence. Knowing that 86 percent of people join churches through the influence of their family and friends, we prayed with that information in mind.[1] The time was going by slowly as we kept tackling the problem in prayer.

Periodically we sang to keep our focus intact and our faith engaged. We read scriptures that reinforced the promises of God to save our loved ones. These activities fueled the slow fire that was building toward our breakthrough. As we pressed into God, some people, including myself, began to pace up and down as Elisha did when he prayed for the dead son of the Shunammite woman to be restored to life (2 Kings 4:32–35). The pacing created a sharp focus and a rhythm that gave us the sense that we were trying to break something that was resisting the will of God. We kept it up until around noon, when the fire of prayer was hot.

We all felt like something had broken in the spirit realm. Whatever demonic force was hindering men from joining our congregation was broken that day. There was nothing holy or magical about it happening at the noon hour. That just happened to be the time when the spiritual resistance opposing God's desire for men to join Christ Church was unseated. Our prayer of agreement was really an act of warfare.

> **Faith carries the force of demonstration
> or proof of its existence in a situation.**

The very next day several new men came to the service and freely gave their hearts to the Lord when the invitation was given. In fact, many of the men are still with us some twenty-two years later. Beginning that Sunday and ever since, several thousand men have called Christ Church their home. When people visit our church and remark about the large percentage of men, I smile because I remember that day when the tiny congregation and I exercised the power found in the prayer of agreement. It took the efforts of a team of kneeling warriors huddled in prayer to secure the title deed of our request.

SECURING THE TITLE DEED

The prayer of agreement is not simply getting a couple of guys to pray with you about a pressing need. It requires faith to secure the things asked of God. In the first verse of Hebrews chapter 11 we learn, "Now faith is being sure of what we hope for and certain of what we do not see." The meaning of faith is best captured by an acronym: Full Assurance In The Heart. However, when you look at the role of faith in the prayer of agreement, the need to develop a holy confidence—an assurance that God is willing to grant your request—must first occur in prayer.

The phrase *title deed* is among the meanings of the word "certain" found in verse 1 of Hebrews chapter 11. It is the Greek word *elegchos* (pronounced *el-eng-khos*), which also means proof, evidence, and assurance. According to the *eminent* Greek scholar Marvin R. Vincent, the word *elegchos* "adds to the simple idea of assurance a suggestion of influences operating to produce conviction which carries the force of demonstration. The word often signifies a process of proof or demonstration."[2] Applying this meaning to the realm of faith, we learn that faith carries the force of demonstration or proof of its existence in a situation.

Title deed or *title*, as we term it today, is the legal proof of property ownership. The writer wants us to see that when genuine faith is at work, it labors to secure the title deed so that whatever is being sought in prayer is sure to follow.

> **The place of agreement is the place
> where the will of God is paramount.**

In the arena of prayer there will come a time during your intercession when you know that you know that what is being sought from God has been given. That experience, which is very subjective and hard to describe, is akin to you receiving the title deed or proof God has done what you've requested. You will no longer have to labor in prayer. It has been done.

Even though you may not see the manifestation immediately, you have received the title deed in that moment in prayer.

When our small congregation prayed for more men, we received the title deed around noon that Saturday—when the fires of prayer reached their hottest. The feeling we experienced of a release or something breaking in the spiritual realm is just another way of saying we received the title deed. Whether you're praying alone or with a team, the goal must be to use your faith to get the title deed of the thing being prayed for.

THE PLACE OF AGREEMENT

When a team of kneeling warriors gathers for prayer, something powerful happens the moment they settle in the place of agreement. You will know when you've arrived at the place of agreement, because Jesus said, "For where *two or three* come together in my name, there am I with them" (Matt. 18:20, emphasis added). The place of agreement is the place where the will of God is paramount. Each member in the prayer huddle desires the will of God above their own personal ambition or goal. This place of agreement is not a physical place. It is a spiritual resolve characterized by selflessness where the participants unanimously exalt God's preference and pleasure.

The place of agreement is best understood when Paul accepted God's answer to his prayer even though it was not the answer he wanted to hear. After Paul prayed three times for the thorn to be taken from him, the Lord said to Paul, "My grace is sufficient for you, for my power is made perfect in weakness. Therefore I will boast all the more gladly about my weaknesses, so that Christ's power may rest on me" (2 Cor. 12:9). The moment Paul accepted God's will, even though it was contrary to his own, he entered the place of agreement. God's power rested on him. The place of agreement is the place of power!

When a group of warriors are huddled in prayer, they all step into the place of agreement as they submit themselves totally to the will of God. At that point the reality of Jesus's statement becomes apparent when He said, "...there am I with them." It's as if Jesus joins the prayer team when everyone willingly surrenders to the will of God. Prayers voiced from that place of agreement are easily answered by God because He knows that the warriors are poised to do whatever He commands them to do or go wherever He commands them to go. There is no resistance in their hearts toward the will of God despite whatever adjustment the warrior may need to make to appropriately carry out the Master's orders. And because of the warriors' total submission to God, He has no desire to withhold the request they voiced in prayer.

On a practical level there are a number of items that must be in order to enter into the place of agreement when you gather with a team of kneeling warriors. Let's explore them so you can quickly begin enjoying the benefits of praying in groups or with a prayer partner. Each item is taken directly from Jesus's words about the practice of the prayer of agreement.

> Again, I tell you that if two of you on earth agree about anything you ask for, it will be done for you by my Father in heaven. For where two or three come together in my name, there am I with them.
> —MATTHEW 18:19–20

Be comfortable in the prayer group.

Praying with someone is a uniquely private and spiritual matter. To open your heart and make a personal request known to the other person, you must feel comfortable with them. I don't mean that you have to be great friends or have a long-standing relationship. I do mean that you must be assured there are no hidden motives or agenda other than their willingness to help you bring your concern before a loving God. Since the focus is on the prayer of agreement, which often includes matters beyond the scope of one person's needs, each member must feel comfortable with the others or at a minimum with the group leader. This is essential to seeing eye to eye with someone about an important matter in affirming the answer being sought is indeed the will of God.

> **Without that level of comfort, praying together is futile and powerless.**

I am a member of a monthly prayer group consisting of area clergy and Christian leaders. The sole goal of the group is to pray for revival to break out in the New Jersey region. Although the topic is a shared desire by all attendees, we didn't experience effectiveness in prayer until we began having times of fellowship with one another. After the members became comfortable with each other, participating in the prayer of agreement became easy.

God has wired human beings with the desire to feel a sense

of belonging. We must know that the people we're with genuinely care for us, respect us, and want what's best for us.

Without that level of comfort, praying together is futile and powerless. When the other leaders of my monthly prayer group began to learn each other's names, the churches they represent, and information about one another's families, we were quickly able to enter the place of agreement each time we gathered for prayer.

If you already know the people with whom you're planning to pray with, you will more easily be able to enter the place of agreement.

Communicate your need.

One clear benefit of the prayer of agreement is to have a fellow warrior band with you in prayer. But your need must be communicated clearly and humbly. This calls for vulnerability on your part. You need to be able to admit when something is bothering you or something is amiss in your life. I've had to humbly request on many occasions that my prayer partner join me in asking God for help with a dilemma one of my children was facing. Other times my need for wisdom in how to handle a matter with one of my leaders was the subject of our prayer time. I recall asking for prayer to withstand media critics reporting on the development plans for our church. This level of vulnerability was uncomfortable to me at first, but I got through it because my prayer partner made it easy for me to open my heart.

No one ever asks for prayer when things are going well. We solicit the help of God when facing crises, emotionally draining trials, or painful incidents. When one of our leaders was diagnosed with cancer, we formed a prayer team to pray for the healing of this precious brother. We regularly agreed in prayer for his recovery, the strengthening of his family, and the maintenance of his faith toward God throughout this ordeal. We would not have been able to enter into the prayer of agreement unless he plainly communicated his need to us. At this writing his health has not been totally restored, so we are still huddled in prayer.

> **Prayer is not a magic wand we wave over our painful circumstances so everything becomes instantly wonderful.**

The prayer of agreement is not an unspoken prayer request. When a team of kneeling warriors gather to do battle against the forces of darkness, they need to be entrusted with a specific order. They have to take a specific problem before the Lord, which requires that the need be clearly communicated to them.

Agree on the meaning of agreement.

Just as Navy SEAL teams must live by the principle of teamwork, kneeling warriors must live by the principle of agreement. Our power lies in our ability to walk and live in agreement with one another. Jesus taught that the Father answers prayers asked by people who are in agreement with each other. The Greek word for "agree" is transcribed into the English word *symphony*. This word captures the sound when music is played in complete accord. The notes do not create discord with one another, but a beautiful resonance occurs.

I don't want to misrepresent prayer here. There are some stories that don't have a happy ending but still offer teachable moments. Such is the case with Debbie and John. This couple had been married for about eighteen years. They came to see me after a few years of difficulty. Their relationship had become so strained they couldn't even have a peaceful conversation with one another. *Contempt* is the best word I can use to describe how they felt about each other. As I listened and offered advice about their need to walk in agreement, they both bristled. Neither of them wanted to bear the responsibility of being in agreement with the other. Apparently they felt that their marriage was not worth fighting for.

Prayer is not a magic wand we wave over our painful circumstances so everything becomes instantly wonderful. Prayer can facilitate miracles even in the realm of relationships, yet the human factor plays a critical role. The parties, at least one of them, must want to agree with God. Agreement with the Lord and then one another is a critical foundation to answered prayers. Debbie and John eventually divorced.

Quite obviously there are equally important restrictions to ensuring agreement, as there are positive indicators to signal when agreement has been reached. The request being voiced must honor Christ. Whatever is being sought should be good and reasonable for the one for whom the request has been made. Prayers of agreement must take into account the importance of the preservation of the will of God. The prayer should also be in keeping with the teachings of Scripture. If you cannot imagine

Jesus saying amen—which means "so be it"—at the end of the prayer, that prayer should not be uttered privately or publicly. It is a prayer that lacks the elements that constitute agreement.

> **The place of agreement is a place where Jesus would feel comfortable asking you to pray with Him about that matter.**

The ultimate way to know whether a request meets the test of agreement is when you are certain Jesus would feel at home in your prayer group. I mean He must feel the same level of passion to pray for the request as you do. If Jesus cannot affirm your request with the same zealousness as if it is His own, that prayer should not be introduced as a request worthy of others presenting it to God.

The place of agreement is a place where Jesus would feel comfortable asking you to pray with Him about that matter. This is what He did in the Garden of Gethsemane. He invited Peter, James, and John to pray with Him about His coming crucifixion. That is the best picture of agreement one can ever see. The three men willingly agreed to intercede alongside Jesus in His hour of need. But as the account went, they fell asleep and He ended up praying by Himself. Apart from that sad reality, we did learn what the picture of agreement ought to look like.

The joy of answered prayer

The reward of walking, living, and praying in agreement with one another is answered prayers. When that occurs, kneeling warriors are thrilled, and at the same instance God is pleased to reward us. Our heavenly Father wants to please us, and we have discovered we're pleasing Him whenever we pray in agreement with one another. This circle of joy is perpetuated as we continue living in community around the principle of agreement.

The joy of answered prayer leads us to keep praying corporately with one another. If you have not known or recognized these four awesome benefits of corporate prayer, I encourage you to find a strong prayer group that keeps Jesus's plan for this generation as their focus. Once you find it, join it without hesitation. The early church understood the principle and practice of group prayer. They became comfortable with group prayer because their individual and corporate needs were freely communicated in a way that made agreement easy. The end result was that their requests were heard and answered by the Lord. They joyously guarded the practice because they saw the power it produced.

THE WARRIORS ASSEMBLED

There are a host of benefits that come along with belonging to a local church. You get the firsthand opportunity to experience community. This is where the deepest part of you connects with the deepest part of others within the congregation. The fact that you and the other members have a relationship with Christ creates an automatic connection that in many cases runs deeper than the one you have with your own biological family. To experience community is also to experience a sense of belonging. You feel at home in the relationships that have formed. This internal connection awakens the deepest emotions in you. You throw your energy, resources, and skills into the church's vision because you want to see it fulfill its calling and purpose. You love to see your pastor's face as he beams from ear to ear with the satisfaction of fulfilling his calling through that local church. In the same breath, if the church hurts or the pastor is suffering from a difficult trial, you find yourself weeping or vigilant in prayer for breakthrough to occur.

When a crisis occurs, there's no time to learn the lessons of warfare praying. You must have already learned how to engage God on a private level as a kneeling warrior.

These kinds of feelings prompted the church in Jerusalem to gather the kneeling warriors for a protracted time of intercession. Acts chapter 12 opens with the sobering fact that King Herod just had James put to death with the sword. This horrible act pleased the Jews. To curry more favor with the Jewish community, Herod arrested Peter with the hope of bringing him to the same fate after the Passover. The church automatically went into warfare mode because the Scripture said, "...but the church was earnestly praying to God for him" (v. 5).

When a crisis occurs, there's no time to learn the lessons of warfare praying. You must have already learned how to engage God on a private level as a kneeling warrior. That way when a public crisis arises, each intercessor has earned their stripes. The church then becomes a battalion of kneeling warriors. This is exactly what happened in Jerusalem that day. The congregation went into crisis mode. Everyone knew the importance of Peter relative to the spiritual health, purpose, and vitality of their congregation. He was one of the original twelve apostles. He walked with Jesus for the entirety of His earthly ministry. He had firsthand knowledge of the Lord. He was ordained in the ministry by Christ Himself. There were things Peter witnessed and lived and could impart to the Jerusalem congregation simply because he was one of the original twelve. Losing him would have been a major loss to the body of Christ and more particularly the church at Jerusalem.

The prayer of agreement had to be employed. In his book *The Power of a City at Prayer* my friend Dr. Mac Pier describes the mind-set of the intercessors when they assemble: "They pray in desperation and in unity; it is sustained; their praying is inspired by the Spirit."[3] Such was the case with the members of the Jerusalem church. People had assembled at different homes to pour out their hearts to God for Peter's release. No one was uncomfortable with the idea of meeting for prayer with the rest of believers. The need was simple. They all knew what it was. Peter had to be set free by the Lord. A miracle was needed. God had to show up big-time. Everyone was in total agreement. Peter's release was the prayer topic and prayer goal. Some people gathered at Mary's house since it was large (Acts 12:12).

While the church was praying, God was at work in the prison cell. An angel visited Peter while he was sleeping in his cell, bound with two chains, and guards stood their posts nearby. The angel woke up Peter, removed his feet and hands from the chains, and stealthily walked him out of the prison. As this was happening, Peter thought he was dreaming. Once outside he realized that this supernatural release was really happening. He went to Mary's house and experienced this reception:

> But Peter kept on knocking, and when they opened the door and saw him, they were astonished. Peter motioned with his hand for them to be quiet and described how the Lord had brought him out of prison. "Tell James and the brothers about this," he said, and then he left for another place.
>
> —Acts 12:16–17

The kneeling warriors were at the place of agreement, as they cried to God for Peter's release. Yet they were astonished to see him standing in Mary's house. Why? Many times when we pray both individually or in a group, we have an idea in our mind about how God is going to answer our prayers. Such was the case with the early church. They sought God by faith for Peter's release from prison, but they had their own thoughts about how he would be freed. Let God decide how He wants to answer our prayers. Our job is to enter into prayer having an unshakable faith in our heavenly Father.

The joy of answered prayer caused the people at Mary's house to release shouts of praise and thanksgiving. Peter had to quiet them down because it was not yet public knowledge that he had been supernaturally released from Herod's clutches. Plus he did not want the Roman soldiers to discover where he was and more importantly that he had escaped. After they quieted down, he told the intercessors of his experience with the angel of the Lord. He also asked them to tell James—the senior leader of the church at Jerusalem—and the other elders and apostles of his supernatural release. They would want to know this good news as soon as possible.

> **The benefits of private prayer are tremendous, and we must continue our private devotional lives, but we cannot ignore the benefits associated with the prayer of agreement, which are only manifested in a group.**

Scripture then captures Peter's final action after communicating to this prayer group: "And then he left for another place." He went into hiding in some underground hideout so the Roman soldiers and King Herod would not be able to locate his whereabouts. Peter's mind-set was that of a warrior. He knew when to encourage the church by letting them know he was safe. Yet he also knew how to hide so he did not tempt God by walking around boldly declaring his supernatural release from prison.

I believe there are a lot of things God wants to do for His church today that may require absolute spiritual militancy and aggressiveness in prayer. Many times this kind of vigilance in intercession requires you to agree with someone else in prayer. The benefits of private prayer are tremendous, and we must continue our private devotional lives, but we cannot ignore the benefits associated with the prayer of agreement, which are only manifested in a group. Add to your life the value of group prayer, and you'll forever be thankful of the rewards you're sure to reap.

I recall a grieving woman who came to me for prayer over her failing marriage. She had been married for almost twenty years. Although her husband came home every night, he had become comfortable keeping himself emotionally distant. In her mind the marriage was a farce, but she did not know what to do. We spent some time praying together asking God for wisdom. From what the husband had insistently communicated to his wife, everything was fine. He insisted his wife's perceptions of the marriage were misguided.

As we prayed, it became clear to me that some dark secret was afoot in the husband's life. For some odd reason the Holy Spirit was not revealing it to me or the wife, as we agreed in prayer. Yet as we continued praying, thoughts of her need to hire a private investigator kept coming to my mind. I shared this thought with her. She heeded my advice. To her surprise, the investigator gave her undeniable proof that her husband had had a girlfriend and a five-year-old love child across town. It was like he was living out a Lifetime movie. No one knew about his double life until the prayer of agreement revealed a course of action to take. Quite obviously she had no recourse but to divorce him.

If you're facing a heavy load or an intense trial, don't try to lift it or endure it by yourself. Your need for relief and breakthrough is not selfish. The legendary intercessor and author Andrew Murray writes, "Desire is the secret power that moves the whole world of living men, and directs the course of each. And so desire is the soul of prayer."[4] Let your desire for God's help move you to assemble a team of kneeling warriors that will agree with you in prayer. You will then know by firsthand experience the power of being a part of a huddle of kneeling warriors.

Chapter 8

IT'S TIME TO
BE DEPLOYED!

A FRIEND RECOUNTED A CHILDHOOD STORY TO ME that shaped his self-image forever. He had been humiliated as an eight-year-old boy as he walked home from school. The class bully, egged on by others, snatched his glasses off his face. Afraid to retaliate, Jose walked home crying. His father, a former soldier in the Marine Corps, asked him why he was crying. Instead of giving him the expected sympathy and "it's going to be alright, son" speech, his father told him, "Go get your stuff, and don't come home until you have your glasses!"

He then called Jose's brother, who was about ten years old and said, "Go with Jose. Make sure he gets his stuff back, but let him handle the matter himself."

Jose feared his dad's reaction more than the bully if he didn't retrieve his glasses. He found the bully gloating over his earlier assault. When I asked Jose what happened, he smiled and said, "It wasn't pretty, but I got my stuff back!"

That childhood lesson left an indelible mark upon Jose. He learned to never cower in fear. He learned that there's a time when you have to stand up for what is right and good no matter how contrary it is to your nature to do so. Today Jose holds a black belt in judo and has no trouble getting his stuff back from anybody. I'm not advocating violence here. What I am pointing out is that if you never become deployed in spiritual warfare, you will end up becoming a discouraged soldier who forever goes through drills and combat exercises but never experiences war firsthand. At some point in your life you will have to draw a line in the sand, and when the devil approaches that line— much less crosses it—you automatically go into warfare mode. Your destiny and valuables must be protected at all times.

In the 2006 movie *Annapolis* Jake Huard, a cocky recruit to the Naval Academy, is confronted and challenged in his effort to become an officer in the US Navy. His main adversary is Midshipman Lieutenant Cole, who is unyielding and heartless in his expectations of Jake. Unlike other officers at the academy, Cole is a battle-seasoned marine. In one of their confrontations Lt. Cole says to Jake, "Private, you're just playing soldier like most of these officers here at the Academy, but I've been a soldier. I've been in real combat."[1] This strong statement helps underscore the difference between theory and practice, between concept and reality, and between *playing* a kneeling warrior and *being* a kneeling warrior.

THE INTERCESSOR'S MISSION

The way that Navy SEALS look forward to their day of deployment, kneeling warriors should look forward to receiving their assignment. After the SEAL team members are briefed on their mission, their hearts are mixed with anxiety and adrenaline as the day of deployment approaches. Intercessors share the same mixed feelings. Yet their courage remains intact because of their needed role in the spiritual war for the souls of men. Ezekiel reminds the nation of Israel of the mission and necessity of God's intercessors when he prophesied, "I looked for a man among them who would build up the wall and stand before me in the gap on behalf of the land so I would not have to destroy it, but I found none" (Ezek. 22:30).

THE ROLE OF INTERCESSION

As always God was in search for someone who wanted to be a soldier and not someone who simply wanted to play the part of a soldier. He searched for an intercessor who would stand before Him. We will learn later in this chapter that one of the roles of an intercessor is to be a representative for God before the people.

To understand the function of spiritual representation and advocacy, let's see how it's used in two portions of Scripture. First, in the Book of Isaiah the term is used in seeking justice on another's behalf. "Then the Lord saw it, and it displeased Him that there was no justice. He saw that there was no man, and wondered that there was no *intercessor*; therefore His own arm brought salvation for Him; and His own righteousness, it sustained Him" (Isa. 59:16, NKJV, emphasis added). God noticed that the people had no representative or advocate to solicit justice on their behalf. So in His wisdom He sent Jesus to be our advocate. The role of an intercessor is much like that of an attorney. The lawyer's job is to represent his client before the courts by advocating on their behalf.

One of the roles of an intercessor is to be a representative *for God* before the people.

Second, God was upset with His people and was unwilling to listen to them, so He said to Jeremiah, "Therefore do not pray for this people, nor lift up a cry of prayer for them, nor make *intercession* to Me; for I will not hear you" (Jer. 7:16, NKJV, emphasis added). Here we see the purpose of intercession is to act as an intermediary or representative of the people before God.

THE MODES OF INTERCESSION

The function of the intercessor must be examined in more detail to understand *how* God wants you to execute this role in your life. I have discovered that when I'm in deep intercession, there are three distinct modes of my prayers. They are noticeably different from one another. Either I'm wrestling, reasoning, or birthing something as I pray.

Intercessors wrestle.

There are times I feel I'm advocating for someone's needs but sense strong opposition. During such times prayer seems difficult; it feels choppy and lacks rhythm and ease—the opposite of sweet communion with God. During these times I feel like I'm wrestling with the enemy of my soul as I pursue God's help. This image can be seen in Paul's description of how Epaphras wrestled in prayer for the people at Colosse to be anchored in the will of God (Col. 4:12–13). Paul actually used the word *wrestling* to describe how Epaphras attempted to unseat the powers of darkness that were working to weaken the confidence, certainty, and assurance of God's will in the people's lives. This mode of intercession is the heart of spiritual warfare. This is spiritual combat.

This phase of intercession must be characterized by persistence. Stay the course in prayer by daily bringing your concern before God. Just as Paul prayed three times for the thorn to be removed from him (2 Cor. 12:8), maintain your vigilance in prayer until the matter is resolved or until God tells you to leave it alone. A. B. Simpson—the founder of the Christian Missionary Alliance denomination—unearthed vigilance as "the best rule about prayer: to pray until we understand the mind of the Lord about it [the matter], and get sufficient light, direction, and comfort to satisfy our hearts....As soon as the assurance comes, we should stop praying, and henceforth everything should be praise."[2]

Intercessors reason.

Other times when I am interceding I feel as if I'm reasoning with God. One such time after I had graduated with my master's in engineering and couldn't find a job in my field, I was at my wit's end as to what to do while holding down various low-paying positions in menial jobs. I told God that I was prepared to do whatever He wanted me to do. I reasoned aloud in prayer: "God, if You want me to work in this spaghetti factory for the rest of my life, I will. And I will not complain any more. Just tell me what You want from me, God. I just want to please You." I knew I was connecting with God in a deep and meaningful way. He had my heart, and I had His. I wanted His will above my satisfaction or pleasure. And He knew it because of how I reasoned in prayer that His will would be totally acceptable to me. This is how Abraham prayed when he represented the cities of Sodom and Gomorrah (Gen. 18:22–33). He reasoned that God should not destroy the city if there are even ten righteous people living there.

> **Just as Paul prayed three times for the thorn to be removed from him (2 Cor. 12:8), maintain your vigilance in prayer until the matter is resolved or until God tells you to leave it alone.**

In this mode of intercession Abraham reasoned with God solely on the grounds of God's word and character. He prayed, "'May the Lord not be angry, but let me speak just once more. What if only ten can be found there?' He [the Lord] answered,

'For the sake of ten, I will not destroy it'" (v. 32). Abraham's intercession was like an attorney reasoning with a judge on behalf of his client. Similarly when you are engaged in this mode of prayer, find a portion of Scripture that clearly communicates God's action, character, or personality and reason with God on that premise alone.

Intercessors give birth.

The third form of intercession is a birthing mode. During this type of prayer session I sense I must give birth to a promise of God. The prophet Isaiah uses a woman travailing with labor pains as a metaphor for birthing a promise of God (Isa. 66:8). When I pray in this mode, I feel like I'm carrying one of God's promises in my heart and that it requires labor and travail to be released from heaven. My prayer is like a woman pushing to give birth to a baby.

THE FUNCTION OF INTERCESSION

Regardless of the mode of intercession, the intercessor carries out specific functions and duties in his intercessory capacity. Let's understand them so you will be more comfortable and effective in your mission to represent people before God.

Intercessors are forerunners.

Marlinda and I planted Christ Church with just six other people. I was only twenty-four years old and worked full-time as an environmental engineer and part-time as a pastor. Those early years were rough as I tried to juggle the responsibilities of both my day job and my passion. I had to battle both emotional and spiritual issues as the church developed. After three years or so we averaged only twenty to twenty-five people a week in worship. I began to wrestle with the question: Am I called to be a pastor? I was teetering on the brink of failure. It was particularly unsettling because I had never failed at anything in my life before this, but this pastoring thing was getting the best of me. That evening I was scheduled to join my prayer partner, Loretta Taylor, for a time of intercession.

Loretta, who has since gone home to be with the Lord, was an elderly minister who had served for about twenty-five to thirty years. We met through a mutual friend about a year prior, and she adopted me as her spiritual son. I was obliged to play that role particularly because I was so inexperienced as a pioneering pastor, young husband, and new father. We regularly prayed together and had become good friends.

One evening as I was driving to Loretta's home, my mind was consumed with the thought that I was a failure as a pastor. I reasoned that the best thing I could do for the congregation was quit. I hadn't even told Marlinda what I had been struggling with. I was too embarrassed.

When I reached her home, I greeted Loretta with a smile and all the superficial gestures that give a sense that "all is well." I was too ashamed and too immature to know how to be real with her or anyone else, even those who could help me. Before we began praying, to my surprise Loretta had prepared a small foot-washing ceremony. Tucked out of sight behind the sofa, Loretta had a pitcher of water, a towel, and a bucket in which I would eventually place my feet. I knew about foot washing from John chapter 13 but had never been on the receiving end of the experience. I felt really awkward. Still I removed my shoes and socks and rolled up my pants as I was told.

Loretta shared that she was going to wash my feet as a symbol of service and deliverance. I listened. As she poured water on my feet, she began to pray. It was no ordinary prayer. It was a passion-filled prayer that only a seasoned intercessor could deliver. The words came from deep inside her soul. As I listened to her prayer, I realized that God had told her something about me, and she was now representing me before God. The Lord had revealed the secret of my heart to this kneeling warrior. She knew I was secretly wrestling with the thought of quitting the ministry because I saw myself as a failure.

> **Intercessors must have and exemplify moral courage. They are forerunners of repentance, confession of sin, and all that is needed to turn people's hearts toward the Lord.**

She started praying that God would break every thought of failure the enemy had planted in my heart and mind. As she prayed, tears started welling up from deep within me and spilling into the bucket of water. Something was being broken over my life. Loretta had been a forerunner in the areas of spiritual intimacy. She kept praying for my breakthrough and deliverance, and I kept on crying. When she stopped pouring the water and started drying my feet, I knew I would never be the same again.

That night I learned firsthand that intercessors are

forerunners. Loretta prayed me back to God's original intent and purpose for my life because she enjoyed living in that place of certainty regarding the will of God for her life. It has been twenty-two years since those prayers of deliverance came over my soul, and I can honestly say I have never wrestled with the ideas of failure since. Nor have I resigned from my calling as a pastor.

Like Ezekiel, Loretta demonstrated one role of a deployed intercessor. Intercessors build up the wall, which simply infers that they restore broken relationships between people and God. The context in which the phrase "build up the wall" was spoken is at the heels of God's search for a leader, a moral influencer, or a forerunner of righteousness. God was looking for "a man"—a leader or a forerunner—who would "build up the wall" (Ezek. 22:30). The Lord was unsuccessful. He did not find anyone who was willing and able to help turn the tide of national corruption. Hebrew scholar Frank E. Gaebelein comments on this verse with this thought: "The current context argues that there was no person to take the lead and lead the nation into confession and a resulting righteous life among the people that would turn away God's wrath."[3] Intercessors must have and exemplify moral courage. They are forerunners of repentance, confession of sin, and all that is needed to turn people's hearts toward the Lord.

Building up the wall is about restoration of the people's relationship and connection with Almighty God. If an intercessor is to pray for others and their city to turn to the Lord, that intercessor must already be enjoying the blessings that righteousness produces in the life of a warrior for Christ. Our power in prayer stems from us having a right relationship with God. This is only possible when *we* enjoy the sweet aroma of confession and the perfume of repentance is always about *our* person. These elements are the foundation to intimacy and power with God. E. M. Bounds writes, "The men who have most fully illustrated Christ in their character, and have most powerfully affected the world for him, have been men who spent much time with God as to make it a notable feature of their lives."[4]

If the work of the intercessor is supposed to have a positive impact on the world, that intercessor must see himself as a forerunner of God's desires. Intercessors must have enjoyed and still enjoy the blessings of God so that they can pray down the very thing they know firsthand to be good for everybody. The intercessor should be able to guide people to the presence of God no matter how far away the people may be at that present moment.

> **The task of the intercessor is to close the opening, repair the break, and plug up the holes that exist in people's relationships with God.**

Intercessors are representatives.

Ezekiel prophesied that God had been looking for someone who would "stand before me in the gap" (Ezek. 22:30). The word *gap* in this verse means "breach" or "breaking forth." It is also found in one other place in the Book of Ezekiel; as he scolded the prophets on their poor behavior, Ezekiel prophesied, "You have not gone up to the *breaks* in the wall to repair it for the house of Israel so that it will stand firm in the battle on the day of the LORD" (Ezek. 13:5, emphasis added). The Hebrew word for "breaks" is the same word used for "gap," which is seen in the definition "breach." The meaning characterizes an opening that has not been closed, a break that has not been repaired, or a hole that remains unplugged.

The task of the intercessor is to close the opening, repair the break, and plug up the holes that exist in people's relationships with God. To do that, the intercessor must represent the people before God and represent God before the people. Intercessors are representatives. They must know the challenges of the people so that they can cry out before God and be heard. This will lead to their transformation. At the same time they must cry out to God for the people to hear and obey God. This latter representation includes the intercessor's request of God to send the people shepherds after His own heart. These shepherds will teach the people how to walk in the ways of the Lord.

The intercession of Abraham for Sodom is a wonderful example of how an intercessor functions as a representative for the people before God and for God before the people. The dual role of an intercessor to function as a representative is captured with these words:

> Then the LORD said, "Shall I hide from Abraham what I am about to do? Abraham will surely become a great and powerful nation, and all nations on earth will be blessed through him...."
> Then the LORD said, "The outcry against Sodom and Gomorrah is so great and their sin so grievous that I will go down and see if what they have done

is as bad as the outcry that has reached me. If not,
I will know."

—Genesis 18:17–18, 20–21

God poured out His complaint to Abraham. He expressed His unhappiness with the sinfulness of Sodom and Gomorrah. It had reached the point where something drastic had to be done. God openly confessed that He would address their reckless behavior, but He shared His initial step of investigation with Abraham. All of God's words conveyed that Abraham functioned as His representative. In other words God was saying: "Abraham, judge what I'm thinking about doing. Let me hear your thoughts."

At that point we are told, "…but Abraham remained standing before the LORD" (v. 22). There in the presence of God Abraham now represents the people. He reasoned that God wouldn't destroy the city if there were fifty righteous people living there. The way Abraham and God went back and forth in this intercessory dialogue shows us how an intercessor is to argue the people's case before God. We are to ask God to withhold His wrath. Soldiers are deployed in battle so more lives are spared than lost. Intercessors are tasked with the same goal. We are in the business of sparing lives by requesting God's intervention, protection, and mercy in the lives of people.

Intercessors defend the land.

Intercessors are tasked with defending the land. Ezekiel indicated that God was looking for someone who would stand before Him *in the gap on behalf of the land.* As intercessors intercede for God's promises to come to pass, they are defending the integrity of the nation they are praying about. As Jeremiah prophesied, "Seek the peace and the prosperity of the city to which I have carried you" (Jer. 29:7), the clarity of what it means to defend the land is more easily understood. The country in which you live and pray for should be thankful you have been deployed to defend it as an intercessor. The defense is evident as the level of peace increases in that nation as you maintain a commitment to pray for it.

The defense is also seen as the nation's level of economic prosperity improves as a reflection of your prayers. The mindset of kneeling warriors cannot be the same as civilians. We are not to bicker about politics even though we ought to stay informed. We must not become partisan in our intercession. Our interest is in defending the land—the whole land. That means we are concerned about Democrats, Republicans, and Independents honoring God, having their needs met, and having an opportunity to receive Christ.

As a pastor I am acutely aware that some of my members are Democrats while others are Republicans, and still others are Independents. If I were to publicly choose sides, I would divide my congregation and by so doing alienate others from my ministry. My role is to serve all members and challenge them equally to follow me as I follow Christ. The same holds true for intercessors. Our responsibility is not to the president or to our political party, but it is to Almighty God to intercede for the ongoing welfare of our nation. If we honor God the way He prescribes, then the president and all political parties will be happy to have us as citizens in this great nation. C. H. Spurgeon once said, "The man who is mighty in prayer may be a wall of fire around his country, her guardian angel and her shield."[5]

Several years ago I was speaking on the subject of *vision* at a leadership conference in Nigeria when a minister angrily interrupted me with these words: "American, what we need here is not vision. We need money! We have vision!" Can you imagine how out of control this man had to be to interrupt my sermon? So I shouted back at him these words: "Your problem is not money because vision brings in provision. Your problem is that you don't love your country. Ever since I've been visiting, I've not heard one Nigerian pastor say a single positive thing about Nigeria. The Bible teaches that we're supposed to seek the peace and prosperity of the nation in which we live." To my shock that man and most of the one hundred pastors in the meeting fell on their faces before God repenting of their violation of the command to "be watchmen for the nation" who are tasked with seeking its peace, prosperity, and transformation.

> **You will know the sphere of your deployment based on what burdens your soul.**

Intercessors keep watch.

Deployment as an intercessor is when you take your post on the wall as a watchman. In biblical days watchmen—akin to security guards—were assigned to ensure that no intruders tried to enter the city. The word *watchmen* became a metaphor for an intercessor. Isaiah gives us this picture when he prophesied: "I have posted watchmen on your walls, O Jerusalem;

they will never be silent day or night. You who call on the LORD, give yourselves no rest, and give him no rest till he establishes Jerusalem and makes her the praise of the earth" (Isa. 62:6–7).

Our job is to keep watch spiritually for actions, thoughts, and practices that attempt to pull us away from godliness and away from God's original design for us. The scope of our responsibilities is not simply national; it can also be regional or local. You will know the sphere of your deployment based on what burdens your soul. God places burdens on each of our hearts as we maintain openness to the Holy Spirit.

If your primary area of intercession is focused on your city, spend time driving through your city in purposeful prayer. Intercede for the political and business leaders and other important individuals that their lives may be balanced and emotionally healthy. Keeping watch over your city includes guarding your city leaders in prayer so no scandals or other disruptions occur that will bring irreparable harm to the quality of life of its citizens. Ask God to raise up spiritual leaders who will care for all of the citizens within your city. Everyone wants to be loved and cared for in the best possible way. The watchman's job is to pray for the needs to be met so that it becomes easy for the people within your intercessory sphere to easily accept and follow Jesus Christ.

Paul points out the behavior of an intercessor by the name of Epaphras when he said:

> Epaphras, who is one of you and a servant of Christ Jesus, sends greetings. He is always wrestling in prayer for you, that you may stand firm in all the will of God, mature and fully assured. I vouch for

him that he is working hard for you and for those
at Laodicea and Hierapolis.

—COLOSSIANS 4:12–13

Epaphras was keeping watch over the souls of the people
residing in the cities of Colosse, Laodicea, and Hierapolis. He
was burdened for them. As he kept watch, specific needs surfaced to his mind and he labored in prayer that those needs
be met. He did not want the people to stumble over matters of
uncertainty regarding God's will or remain spiritually immature. These particular needs held much of his focus in prayer.

In watching over a city or a family, you must strive to know
their weaknesses and emotional needs. If people's needs are not
adequately addressed, they will do almost anything, including
sin, in an attempt to satisfy their intense cravings and lack.

**You can discern your assignment by being
conscious of two things. What *do you hate
the most? What do you love the most?***

UNDERSTANDING DEPLOYMENT

There are different types of intercessors just as there are different types of prophets. We each have to discover *how* the Holy
Spirit works in us and *what* the Holy Spirit has called us to do.
The *how* and *what* vary from person to person. One assignment
is not better than the other. It's just different. Both are necessary. If you try to take someone else's deployment letter and
make it your own, frustration and failure are sure to occur.

Can you picture Elijah living in the palace of Babylon instead of Daniel? I couldn't, given the personality, mannerisms, and prophetic style of Elijah. Elijah was a wild man who ate food from ravens, drank water from running brooks, called fire down on sacrifices as a showdown of spiritual authority, and killed false prophets who misled people. Daniel, on the other hand, was a statesman who was at peace in the halls of power and skillful in administrating the affairs of government. The two men were powerful in their own rights. The two men were strong men of prayer and fasting. Yet it should be noted that their assignments were different.

You can discern your assignment by being conscious of two things. I will ask you two questions; each will help you identify the type of intercessory deployment God has given to you. First, what do you hate the most? Second, what do you love the most?

What do you hate the most?

The Holy Spirit works through our feelings, emotions, and desires. The feelings of hate are pretty strong. Epaphras hated uncertainty and seeing people waffle back and forth because of spiritual immaturity. The thrust of his intercession was on seeing people grounded in the will of God (Col. 4:12–13). Paul said, "He is *always* wrestling in prayer for you that you may stand firm in all the will of God" (v. 12, emphasis added). The hatred of spiritual ambivalence and uncertainty was a regular topic of prayer for Epaphras.

I do not mean to imply that the only thing Epaphras prayed about was the need for people to be planted in the ways of the Lord. I do recognize his deployment as an intercessor gave him a charge to help others within the region to overcome insta-bility, so he focused on praying for people to be anchored in the will of God. You need to give some thought to the question of what you hate the most, because it may unlock some direction to you regarding your prayer assignment.

What do you love the most?

The apostle John loved to see people live in intimacy with God. He is generally referred to as the apostle of love. In the Gospel of John we read about him leaning back against Jesus as an act of affection (John 13:25). Also, John's Gospel is the only one that captures the intimate act of foot washing. Throughout his three letters—First, Second, and Third John—he spends an inordinate amount of time helping people work through common roadblocks to achieving spiritual intimacy with God. From learning how to confess their sins to God (1 John 1:9), to avoiding the clutches of the world (1 John 2:15), to practicing self-forgiveness (1 John 3:18–20), it's clear the apostle John loved to see people experience intimacy with God.

His ministry of prayer focused on helping people have con-fidence with God (1 John 5:14–15). This is the greatest proof of a spiritually intimate life. If you know you are accepted by God, then your life pleases Him. A life pleasing to God is what John strived to see others experience in his intercession. That's why he taught, "If anyone sees his brother commit a sin that does not lead to death, he should pray and God will give him life" (1 John 5:16).

Ask yourself this question: What do I love the most? The answer will help you hone in on the areas you should spend time interceding about. You may discover how gifted you are in getting wonderful results of answered prayers in those areas.

In his book *Revival Praying* Leonard Ravenhill recounts a prayer he heard a nurse pray at one of his midweek prayer meetings. It impacted him tremendously because it represented an unspoken request of his own heart. He captured it verbatim with these words: "Lord, I don't want to carry burdens others make for me, nor burdens the devil makes for me, nor burdens the church wants to put on me, nor burdens from myself. But I do want to carry the burdens You make for me."[6]

Her prayer sums up the perspective of deployment a kneeling warrior must have in order to stay the course required in developing a lifestyle of intercession. Only the genuine burden of the Lord can keep you focused in prayer. This assignment makes you rise early in the morning to seek the face of your Beloved or even tarry late in the night. Strive to discover the exact burden God has placed on your heart. In so doing you will have an unmistakable passion to fulfill the orders outlined in your deployment letter.

Chapter 9

THE LEGACY OF A KNEELING WARRIOR

CHRIST CHURCH IS A MULTISITE CONGREGATION WITH two locations, which we refer to as the East Campus and West Campus. While it was relatively easy to acquire the East Campus—a historic cathedral in the metropolitan township of Montclair, New Jersey—it was a long and painful experience to secure the West Campus. Each step had to be bathed in prayer because of the many hurdles, roadblocks, and deterrents.

Located about twenty-five miles from our East Campus, our second location in Rockaway, New Jersey, features three large buildings—totaling some 300,000 square feet of space—on 107 picturesque acres. By simply driving onto the property you enter into its serenity of lush trees and flowering hedges and feast upon idyllic sightings of bunnies, deer, and other common wildlife.

You can tell I'm quite proud of this property, but my pride is not based on its size or grandness. This property is a testament to the grace of God and the many years of persistent praying by the congregation. It is a legacy derived from the prayers of our kneeling warriors.

To secure the property we went through almost four years of legal headaches ranging from municipal hearings and threats to seize our property by eminent domain to our filing a lawsuit against the township, and many other painful and costly hurdles. Although the people of Rockaway Township are wonderful individuals, the idea of a large church taking up residence in their small community created much fear and anxiety. So a small faction vigorously fought us at every turn.

The media had a field day. There were at least two hundred newspaper articles written by reporters from national newspapers such as the *New York Times* as well as from reporters at local papers such as *The Daily Record*. Reporters were regularly attending services just to find out how I addressed my congregation during this season and what types of sermons I preached. We weathered the storms of controversy, including adversarial groups levying unfounded accusations against Christ Church and me through social media. Further, while dealing with all of this, I had to continue managing the wide array of challenges associated with pastoring a growing congregation. Needless to say, I was under a tremendous and seemingly unrelenting spiritual attack. If there was ever a time I was in the throes of spiritual warfare, it was then. The public hearings went three years beyond the typical six months an application like ours would generally merit. Then the fight continued an additional three years after receiving approval. In total, we were in the thick fog of the West Campus acquisition for about six years.

> **There are always prizes for winning the battle even in spiritual warfare.**

Now each week as I preach from its pulpit I know firsthand the legacy prayer can achieve. Through intercession our church was able to establish a living and lasting legacy for the next generation of Christ-followers because of the power of prayer.

LEGACY MAKERS

Every warrior wants to come home from the battle with the spoils of war. There are always prizes for winning the battle even in spiritual warfare. When accused of casting out demons by Beelzebub, the prince of demons, Jesus questioned His accusers, "How can anyone enter a strong man's house and *carry off his possessions* unless he first ties up the strong man? Then he can *rob his house*" (Matt. 12:29, emphasis added). Jesus taught that part of the legacy of a kneeling warrior is the possessions he carries off from the camp of the enemy. This warrior has robbed Satan of his precious goods—the souls of men. The spoils of intercession are also the promises of God that have been birthed through prayer.

Kneeling warriors see themselves as legacy makers. There are five marks of a legacy maker. Each mark provides motivation for the intercessor to stay the course of prayer.

1. Legacy makers are focused.

2. Legacy makers surround themselves with encouragement.

3. Legacy makers see themselves as essential.

4. Legacy makers are missional people.

5. Legacy makers care about their legacy.

LEGACY MAKERS ARE FOCUSED

The call to remain vigilant in prayer is difficult at times. There are many distractions—both natural and spiritual. Learning to stay focused on the desired outcome of prayer is what makes vigilance manageable. What is the prayer request? How important is it to receive God's answer? This is part of the inner dialogue of kneeling warriors.

On November 13, 2009, Omar Oyarebu, a member of my congregation of Nigerian descent, received a disturbing call from a family member. His dad, Dr. Kenneth Oyarebu—an American-based physician—was kidnapped while on a visit to Edo State, Nigeria. The gunmen threatened to kill him unless they received the ransom they demanded. Apart from turning to God, Omar didn't know what else to do, so he contacted the Upper Room Community—our church's intercessory prayer group. When he told them the story, this seasoned group of kneeling warriors took this uncommon emergency before the throne of God. Their request was singular in focus: "Lord, return Dr. Oyarebu back to his family without harm and in a miraculous way." They continued praying through the night for this and other requests.

> **The spoils of intercession are also the promises of God that have been birthed through prayer.**

Our intercessors also kept this emergency in focus before the Lord during their individual times of prayer that week. Omar and his family had already begun making arrangements to pay the ransom note even though they were hoping for a miracle. While his uncle was preparing to wire the ransom, he received a call that Dr. Oyarebu had miraculously escaped. No money was wired.[1]

When the Upper Room Community heard the news, the warriors gave a shout of praise to God. This answer came as they remained focused in prayer. Legacies occur as intercessors maintain focus on the reward they are seeking through prayer.

LEGACY MAKERS SURROUND THEMSELVES WITH ENCOURAGEMENT

Most intercessors battle privately. Unlike preaching, singing, or other forms of spiritual ministry, prayer usually happens in isolation and behind closed doors. There are no crowds. There is no one to congratulate you or slap you a high five for your prayer accomplishments. The only audience is God, whom you cannot see.

This means you need to surround yourself with encouragement to avoid ringing the bell. Maybe that's why so many others have rung the bell, removed their helmet, and joined the prayerless society. There are four things I do to encourage myself in prayer. These actions motivate me to stay the course of prayer, where legacies can be produced.

First, I stock my library with good books on the subject of prayer, such as C. H. Spurgeon's book *Lectures to My Students*. I have read the chapter "The Preacher's Private Prayer" in that book at least ten times. Each time I read it, I am encouraged to pray more and to protect the discipline of prayer in my life. Another favorite of mine is Leonard Ravenhill's book *Revival Praying*. This little book has been a friend of mine during dry seasons in my life and ministry. Through the words of this book Ravenhill has told me often, "Stay the course. Keep stoking the fires, and you'll enjoy the flames of revival."

Books are motivators, especially the books written by people who've lived the life of prayer. When you read Norman P. Grubb's book that is simply titled *Rees Howells Intercessor*, there will be no question in your mind that Rees Howells was an intercessor. He ate, slept, and lived prayer to God.

Good books on prayer have been friends to me. Their words have whispered encouragement to my soul. They were like Aaron and Hur to Moses—they lifted my arms when they were sagging under the weight of discouragement. I hope you find this book and others like it to be a friend to you.

Second, I have been encouraged to pray because my soul has been so thirsty for God. Like King David, many nights I cried as I prayed these words: "O God, you are my God, earnestly I seek you; my soul thirsts for you" (Ps. 63:1). I have found praying to be one of my most effective ways to get a fresh drink from the waters of salvation. As I pray for God to reveal His heart and ways to me, I find myself longing to pray more. My desperation for God encourages me to stay spiritually hungry.

Third, encouragement comes as I focus on the blessings that come to the people for whom I've prayed. Answered prayers keep me excited about prayer. I am encouraged when I see problems, trials, and hardships being averted from people for whom I labored in prayer. The fact that God has helped those individuals who would have otherwise been buried under the weight of crisis keeps me excited about prayer.

Fourth, I surround myself with the biographies and testimonies of historic intercessors. These kneeling warriors known only from the pages of history—biblical and contemporary—have encouraged me beyond my imagination by their exploits in prayer. My desire to be an intercessor in my generation is a testament of their legacies. Kneeling warriors such as Martin Luther, Robert Murray M'Cheyne, Father Daniel Nash, Amanda Smith, E. M. Bounds, and biblical characters like Epaphras and Daniel have been motivators to me. Like the writer of Hebrews, I can wholeheartedly say, "Since we are surrounded by such a great cloud of witnesses, let us throw off everything that hinders and the sin that so easily entangles, and let us run with perseverance the race marked out for us" (Heb. 12:1).

These historic intercessors have surrounded me, providing an ongoing source of encouragement to my own attempts to grow as a man of prayer. These four things have proven to be great sources of encouragement to me in maintaining a life of an intercessor.

LEGACY MAKERS SEE
THEMSELVES AS ESSENTIAL

Our nation, like most nations of the world, becomes extremely religious during times of national crisis. I suspect that kind of response is normal to human nature. Praying people are sought out during those critical times. Once the sudden impact of the tragedy subsides, unbelievers tend to hope that spiritually minded people retreat into their own private worlds until the next time they are "really" needed. This is an unfortunate reality we face in our fallen society that otherwise takes umbrage with the mention of God or Jesus in public spaces and places.

To pursue the path that produces a legacy, you must view yourself as a kneeling warrior who is essential to this generation. Intercessors are needed. They are not optional. Where would Charles Finney—the great nineteenth-century American evangelist—have been without the intercessory work of Father Daniel Nash? Finney's evangelistic preaching during the 1800s led upwards of a half million people to Christ.

Father Nash emerged from a cold backslidden state to take up the mantle of prayer. He was a forerunner of Finney's meetings. His function was to locate a humble place for lodging and spend days on his face before God for the souls of people in that city to be converted as Finney preached. This essential role of Father Nash went unseen and unsung, but through his efforts of prayer and fasting hundreds of thousands came to know Christ as their Savior.

Ann E. Brown, one of the powerful intercessors at Christ Church, is frequently heard telling her story about the role prayer played in bringing her entire family to Christ. In the early 1980s, like many American families, Ann was experiencing pain in her marriage. She and Arnold eventually separated to try to sort out what the future would hold for them and their three sons. Ann came to Christ during that ordeal. She also experienced a spirit of prayer. She could not stop interceding for the salvation of her husband and sons, two of whom were drug addicts. Arnold owned a liquor store and a bar in a seedy part of town. The situation looked bleak, almost beyond the grace of God to correct. But Ann learned that nothing is impossible with God. She also knew that if God didn't work a miracle, there would be no way her family would be healed and restored. She took up prayer as an essential part of her life.

Intercessors are needed. They are not optional.

As God would have it, the marriage was healed and Arnold came to Christ. In fact, I remember the day he began coming to Christ Church and how God powerfully impacted him through a personal prophecy I spoke over his life. I saw a man yield himself to the desires of God right before my eyes. It was a powerful and humbling sight to behold. Arnold sold his bar and liquor store and became sold out to Jesus.

Ann kept praying for her sons, and Arnold joined her in prayer. The two sons who were addicts were delivered from drugs, albeit through a lengthy stay in a Christian drug rehabilitation center. Today all three sons are serving the Lord and are powerful in their own right as servants of Christ. Ann and Arnold Brown have been members of Christ Church for more than twenty years, and they are two of the strongest deacons in our ministry. And they are directors of an outreach arm of the church called the Overcomers' Group—a Christian-based program designed to help people find freedom from the bondage of substance abuse and behavioral addictions.

When Ann speaks about the essential benefit of prayer, it comes from a place deep inside her. This intercessor knows without a shadow of a doubt that her role and work in the arena of prayer are essential. She tries to instill this same reality into anyone who comes within earshot.

LEGACY MAKERS
ARE MISSIONAL PEOPLE

We serve a missional God. He *sent* His Son on a mission to die for our sins. Alan Hirsch encourages us to speak of God then as a "missionary God."[2] His actions and desires emerge from a clear sense of purpose and mission. Jesus continued in the same vein by calling us to be a missional people. He said, "Go into all the world and preach the gospel." We have been sent on this mission that ends only when we die; thus it behooves intercessors to be missional in their approach to prayer and praying.

Jesus also gave a missional focus to what His church is to be in its final state when He passionately shared, "My house will be called a house of prayer for all nations" (Mark 11:17). We have been given a missional mandate to build the Lord's house on the foundation of prayer. We must ensure it functions on that very principle going forward. As I have endeavored to adhere to this mandate, I quickly discovered I cannot help people develop a life of prayer without it flowing out of my life. The age-old cliché is found to be accurate once again: you can't take anyone where you have never been.

Kneeling warriors recognize the missional charge of the Great Commission (Matt. 28:19–20) is evangelistic in its thrust while the Prayer Commission's task (Mark 11:17) is discipleship in its requirements. Both responsibilities can only be accomplished if they are viewed as goals to be included in your overall desire to leave behind a legacy for the next generation. A legacy is anything of value handed down from the past. The Prayer Commission charges us to establish the church as a house of prayer in our generation *and* as a legacy for coming generations.

**We have been given a missional
mandate to build the Lord's house
on the foundation of prayer.**

Scripture tells us to "contend for the faith that was once for all entrusted to the saints" (Jude 3). The word *contend* helps us capture the fact that spiritual warfare is required to adhere to the missional goal of the Prayer Commission. Satan is not going to sit idly by and watch us effortlessly build strong intercessors who in turn will easily build strong houses of prayer. It won't happen that way.

> **Great intercessors are great in their personal life of prayer *and* because they've made a significant contribution in helping develop that same quality of intercession in others.**

Rather, we must fight to preserve the legacy of prayer that was handed down to us by the early church. And we must guard that legacy so that we can hand it down to the next generation. This goal can only be upheld when kneeling warriors recognize that one of the fivefold components of their legacy is to view prayer as a missional activity and not simply as God's correspondence system. Stephen Covey, a well-known author, underscores the value of having a legacy in the spiritual dimension of life when he writes:

> There are certain things that are fundamental to human fulfillment.... The essence of these needs is captured in the phrase "to live, to love, to learn, to leave a legacy." The need to live is our *physical* need for such things as food, clothing, shelter, economical well-being, health. The need to love is our *social* need to relate to other people, to belong, to love and to be loved. The need to learn is our *mental* need to develop and to grow. And the need to leave a legacy is our *spiritual* need to have a

sense of meaning, purpose, personal congruence, and contribution.[3]

Great intercessors are great in their personal life of prayer *and* because they've made a significant contribution in helping develop that same quality of intercession in others. Legacy makers think about others. When William Booth, the founder of The Salvation Army, was on his deathbed, he was afforded the generous opportunity to send a free telegraph—the primary means of long-distance communications at the time—to members of The Salvation Army around the world. Booth thought for a few seconds and scribbled his message on a piece of paper. To the operator's surprise there was just a single word on the paper. It was the word *Others*.[4] General Booth wanted to keep the Salvationists—as they were called in those days—so missionally focused that *others* would be their primary objective. This is the word I want to highlight to you as you consider the moral inheritance you want to leave behind. Think of *others*. Become missionally driven to leave a legacy of prayer.

LEGACY MAKERS CARE ABOUT THEIR LEGACY

Billy Graham once said, "Our days are numbered. One of the primary goals in our lives should be to prepare for our last day. The legacy we leave is not just in our possessions, but in the quality of our lives. What preparations should we be making now? The greatest waste in all of our earth, which cannot be recycled or reclaimed, is our waste of the time that God has given us each day."[5] These words are true, and they powerfully convict me to maximize the use of my time not just for earthly reasons but also heavenly ones.

Kneeling warriors shape history as they provide a contribution to others more valuable than money. Spurgeon notes, "A certain preacher, whose sermons converted men by scores, received a revelation from heaven that not one of the conversions was owing to his talents or eloquence, but all to the prayers of an illiterate lay-brother, who sat on the pulpit steps, pleading all the time for the success of his sermon."[6] This unsung hero spent countless hours praying for the effectiveness of his preacher because he valued prayer and cared about the legacy that prayer produces.

The fivefold benefit of a legacy maker is critical in shaping and changing the world through prayer. Your legacy creates a reassuring future to coming generations. One of the sweetest sounds to a troubled heart is to hear these words from a kneeling warrior: "I am praying for you." It is what Jesus said to reassure Simon Peter when He told him that Satan had desired to sift him like wheat. The Master said, "But I have prayed for you, Simon, that your faith may not fail" (Luke 22:32). Peter's future was shaped through the prayer of Jesus. It's our turn now to shape the future of others through our prayers.

We must form a legacy-building plan so the value of prayer is safely passed on to the next generation. As Elijah passed on the value and anointing of a prophet to Elisha, he first gave thought to how this precious legacy could be transferred.

There were several noteworthy elements. First, Elijah valued what God had given him. To be gifted with the ability to speak for God is priceless. It afforded him numerous unique experiences from forecasting a national drought allowed by God to calling fire down from heaven in an effort to stimulate national revival (1 Kings 18). Second, Elijah took the necessary time to develop the ministry gift of prophet within budding prophets through the formation of a school of prophets (2 Kings 2:1–9). You cannot admit to caring about the role of intercession and how it must be imparted to the next generation unless you personally take *time* to instill that value in others. You may not start a school of prayer, but you will mentor others in spiritual warfare whenever the opportunity presents itself.

Effective time management is only seen when you value your time. I once participated in a conference with a few old-timers who valued prayer and intimacy with God. One of the men was staying at the home of the senior pastor rather than a hotel. The pastor was known for his habitual lateness. Prior to the start of each service there was a time of preservice prayer. As chance would have it, the pastor was late once again in leaving his home with his guest. They arrived minutes before the service started, missing preservice prayer. The old man was incensed. He said to the pastor, "In fifty years of ministry I've never missed preservice prayer except for today because of you!" What a testimony of how this seasoned kneeling warrior cared for prayer. Equally important was the poor testimony of how a pastor carelessly guarded his time and how it became evident in his low value of prayer.

The third observation I want to make about Elijah's passing a legacy down to Elisha is Elijah looked for passion to be present in his protégé before he released his priceless gift to him. When Elisha made known to Elijah that the reason he was sticking close to his side those last few days was because he wanted to inherit a double portion of his spirit, Elijah responded with these exact words: "You have asked a difficult thing yet if you see me when I am taken from you, it will be yours—otherwise not" (2 Kings 2:10). The passion Elijah sought for in Elisha before he released a double portion of his anointing was a passion for God, passion for God's people, and a passion to execute the office of the prophet in an exemplary manner.

Elijah's screening of Elisha at this final moment before his supernatural departure to heaven reflected a genuine care about his legacy. This is why Paul gave these instructions to young Timothy: "And the things you have heard me say in the presence of many witnesses entrust to reliable men who will also be qualified to teach others" (2 Tim. 2:2).

> **The passion Elijah sought for in Elisha before he released a double portion of his anointing was a passion for God, passion for God's people, and a passion to execute the office of the prophet in an exemplary manner.**

We must care so much about our legacies that we hand them down only to reliable people. These are people who will treasure this spiritual inheritance and in turn hand them down to others when their time comes. Archbishop Desmond Tutu in his book *God Has a Dream* wrote, "Anything less than God cannot satisfy our hunger for the divine. Not even success. That is why everything else, if we give it our ultimate loyalty—money, fame, drugs, sex, whatever—turns into ashes in our mouths."[7] Our ultimate loyalty should be to Christ and His missional calling on our lives, which includes our quest to pass on the legacy of prayer to others.

Notes

Introduction

1. Charles H. Spurgeon, "A Lecture for Little-Faith," in *Faith in All Its Splendor* (N.p.: Sovereign Grace Publishers, 2006), 11. Viewed at Google Books.

2. C. S. Lewis, *Christian Reflections* (Grand Rapids, MI: Wm. B. Eerdmans Publishing, 1994), 33. Viewed at Google Books.

3. As quoted in Philip M. Taylor, *Global Communications, International Affairs and the Media Since 1945* (New York: Routledge, 1997), 170. Viewed at Google Books.

4. John Bunyan, *The Pilgrim's Progress* (New York: Oxford University Press, 1966), 114.

Chapter 1:
The Making of a Kneeling Warrior

1. As quoted in John Maxwell, *Talent Is Never Enough* (Nashville: Thomas Nelson Inc., 2007), 140–141. Viewed at Google Books.

2. Andrew Bonar, *Robert Murray M'Cheyne* (Carlisle, PA: The Banner of Truth Trust, 1960), 16.

3. Leonard Ravenhill, *Revival Praying* (Minneapolis, MN: Bethany House Publishers, 1984), 59.

4. Jessie Penn-Lewis with Evan Roberts, *War on the Saints*, 9th ed. (New York: Thomas E. Lowe Ltd., 1994), 264. Viewed at Google Books.

5. NavySEALS.com, "SEAL Ethos," http://navyseals.com/ns
-overview/seal-ethos/ (accessed February 11, 2013).

CHAPTER 2:
DON'T RING THE BELL!

1. Mark Kennan, "How to Calculate Velocity in a Fall," Ehow
.com, http://www.ehow.com/how_8102428_calculate-velocity-fall
.html (accessed February 11, 2013).

2. As quoted in Spurgeon, "A Lecture for Little-Faith," in
Faith in All Its Splendor, 11.

3. Desmond Tutu, *God Has a Dream* (New York: Doubleday,
2004), 2.

4. Jennifer Rosenberg, "The War Is Over...Please Come
Out," 20th Century History, About.com, http://history1900s
.about.com/od/worldwarii/a/soldiersurr.htm (accessed February
12, 2013).

CHAPTER 3:
THE WARRIOR'S LIFE

1. As quoted in European Graduate School, "Augustine of
Hippo—Quotes," http://www.egs.edu/library/augustine-of-hippo/
quotes/ (accessed February 13, 2013).

2. Charles H. Spurgeon, *Spurgeon's Sermons*, vol. 2 (1856)
(N.p.: CCEL). Viewed at Google Books.

3. Priscilla Shirer, *He Speaks to Me: Preparing to Hear From
God* (Chicago: Moody Publishers, 2006), 14.

4. A. W. Tozer, *The Pursuit of God* (N.p.: WLC, 2009), 12.

5. Kenneth Wuest, *Word Studies From the Greek New Testament*, vol. 3 (Grand Rapids, MI: Wm. B. Eerdmans Publishing,
2002), 800.

6. E. M. Bounds, *E. M. Bounds on Prayer* (New Kensington,
PA: Whitaker House, 1997), 35–36.

7. C. H. Spurgeon, *Lectures to My Students* (New York:
Sheldon and Company, 1875), 77. Viewed at Google Books.

8. Ole Hallesby, *Prayer* (Minneapolis, MN: Augsburg Fortress, 1994), 91.

9. C. S. Lewis, *The Screwtape Letters* (Old Tappan, NJ: Fleming H. Revell, Co., 1976).

10. Dick Eastman, *The Hour That Changes the World* (Grand Rapids, MI: Chosen Books, 2007), 21.

CHAPTER 4:
THE WEAPONS OF A KNEELING WARRIOR

1. Colin L. Powell, *My American Journey* (New York: Random House, 1995), 20.

2. Ibid., 34.

3. As quoted in R. T. Kendall, *In Pursuit of His Glory* (Lake Mary, FL: Charisma House, 2004), 21.

CHAPTER 5:
WELCOME TO THE SCHOOL OF PRAYER!

1. C. S. Lewis, *The Problem of Pain*, in *The Complete C. S. Lewis Signature Classics* (San Francisco: HarperSanFrancisco, 2002), 406.

2. Dick Eastman, *No Easy Road* (Grand Rapids, MI: Chosen Books, 2003).

3. Charles G. Finney, *Lectures on Revivals of Religion* (New York: Leavitt, Lord, and Co., 1835), 83. Viewed at Google Books.

4. Flavius Josephus, *Antiquities of the Jews*, book 5, http://www.biblestudytools.com/history/flavius-josephus/antiquities-jews/book-5/chapter-10.html (accessed February 15, 2013).

CHAPTER 6:
THE ART OF SPIRITUAL WARFARE

1. John Maxwell, *Be a People Person* (Colorado Springs, CO: David C. Cook, 2007), 164.

2. ThinkExist.com, "George Matthew Adams Quotes," http://thinkexist.com/quotation/there_are_high_spots_in_all_of_our_lives_and_most/207343.html (accessed February 15, 2013).

CHAPTER 7:
THE WARRIORS' HUDDLE

1. C. Peter Wagner, *Church Growth: State of the Art* (Carol Stream, IL: Tyndale House Publishers, 1986), 53.

2. *Vincent's Word Studies in the New Testament*, electronic database. Copyright © 1997 by Biblesoft, s.v. "*elegchos*."

3. Mac Pier and Katie Sweeting, *The Power of a City at Prayer* (Downers Grove, IL: InterVarsity Press, 2002), 68.

4. Andrew Murray, *The Ministry of Intercession* (N.p.: BiblioLife, LLC, 2009), 106.

CHAPTER 8:
IT'S TIME TO BE DEPLOYED!

1. *Annapolis*, directed by Justin Lin (2006; Hollywood, CA: Touchstone Pictures, 2006), DVD.

2. A. E. Thompson, *A. B. Simpson: His Life and Work* (N.p.: Christian Publications, 1960), 188.

3. Frank E. Gaebelein, ed., *The Expositor's Bible Commentary*, vol. 6 (Grand Rapids, MI: Zondervan, 1986), 850.

4. E. M. Bounds, *Power Through Prayer* (New York: Cosimo Classics, 2007), 54.

5. Spurgeon, *Lectures to My Students*, 75.

6. Leonard Ravenhill, *Revival Praying* (Bloomington, MN: Bethany House Publishers, 1962, 2005), 79.

CHAPTER 9:
THE LEGACY OF A KNEELING WARRIOR

1. Gabriel Enogholase, "US-Based Doctor Kidnapped in Edo," *Vanguard*, November 17, 2009, http://www.vanguardngr

.com/2009/11/us-based-doctor-kidnapped-in-edo/ (accessed February 20, 2013); Morrison Hayble, "Trad Ruler Flays Police Over High Rate of Kidnappings," *Nigerian Observer*, http://www .nigerianobservernews.com/26012010/news/insideedo/indexnews6 .html (accessed February 20, 2013).

2. Alan Hirsch, *The Forgotten Ways* (Grand Rapids, MI: Brazos Press, 2006), 129.

3. Stephen R. Covey, A. Roger Merrill, and Rebecca R. Merrill, *First Things First* (New York: Free Press, 1994), 44–45. Viewed at Google Books.

4. "Grad Speech Promotes 'Others,'" *Central Connection*, vol. 37, no. 10, October 2007, 9; http://www.usc.salvationarmy.org/usc/ cc/CenConnOct07.pdf (accessed February 20, 2013).

5. Billy Graham, *Hope for a Troubled Heart* (Nashville: Thomas Nelson, 2011), 179. Viewed at Google Books.

6. Spurgeon, *Lectures to My Students*, 74.

7. Tutu, *God Has a Dream*, 34.

About the Author

D R. DAVID IRELAND IS FOUNDER AND SENIOR PASTOR of Christ Church in Montclair, New Jersey, a six-thousand-member congregation of forty nationalities. Diversity consultant to the National Basketball Association, Dr. Ireland leads chapel services for the New York Giants, New York Jets, and at the US Pentagon. Author of approximately twenty books, Ireland has appeared on *The Dr. Phil Show*, the *CBS Evening News*, and *The 700 Club*. Through his community development corporation he offers a home for victims of domestic violence and a youth leadership institute.

The Rev. Ireland holds an undergraduate degree in mechanical engineering (Fairleigh Dickinson University), a graduate degree in civil engineering (Stevens Institute of Technology), and a master's degree in theology (Alliance Theological Seminary). He has an earned doctorate degree in organizational leadership (Regent University) and has completed post-doctoral work at the University of Pennsylvania. Dr. Ireland was recently appointed as a member of the Governor's Advisory Commission on Faith-Based Initiatives. He also serves on the boards of Nyack College and Alliance Theological Seminary and was an adjunct professor at Drew University. He and his wife, Marlinda, have been married since 1984 and have two adult daughters.

EMPOWERED
TO RADICALLY CHANGE
YOUR WORLD

FREE NEWSLETTERS
TO HELP EMPOWER YOUR LIFE

Why subscribe today?

❏ **DELIVERED DIRECTLY TO YOU.** All you have to do is open your inbox and read.

❏ **EXCLUSIVE CONTENT.** We cover the news overlooked by the mainstream press.

❏ **STAY CURRENT.** Find the latest court rulings, revivals, and cultural trends.

❏ **UPDATE OTHERS.** Easy to forward to friends and family with the click of your mouse.

CHOOSE THE E-NEWSLETTER THAT INTERESTS YOU MOST:

- Christian news
- Daily devotionals
- Spiritual empowerment
- And much, much more

SIGN UP AT: **http://freenewsletters.charismamag.com**